A TEXAS TREASURY OF DUTCH OVEN COOKING

Compiled by the Lone Star Dutch Oven Society

Lone Star Dutch Oven Society Cookbook

First Edition October 1997

Printed by Minuteman Press Ingram Park Place
San Antonio, Texas

ISBN 096779853-1

© 2002 Lone Star Dutch Oven Society and Lodge Manufacturing Company

Table of Contents

The History of Dutch Oven Cooking	5
Overview	7
Buying and Breaking In An Oven	7
Charcoal and Temperature Control	10
Breakfast	15
Main Dishes	
Beef	25
Chicken	49
Fish and Wild Game	85
Pork	93
Side Dishes	111
Soup, Stew, and Chili	125
Bread and Rolls	
Quick Breads	131
Yeast Breads	143
Desserts	
Cakes	163
Desserts	187
Pies and Cobblers	201

Lone Star Dutch Oven Society Cookbook

ABOUT THE LONE STAR DUTCH OVEN SOCIETY (LSDOS)

The Lone Star Dutch Oven Society (LSDOS) was established in the fall of 1994. There were at that time other Dutch oven societies, primarily in the western states. Our founders thought that it was time to get a society started here in Texas that would be open to Texans and non-Texans, who were interested in cooking outdoors with those wonderful old cast iron ovens.

Our LSDOS was patterned after what our founders believed to be the better parts of other Dutch oven societies, but with a truly friendly Texas flair. Granted, our society is still considered young compared with some of the other societies, but it is experienced, as some of our members have been cooking with Dutch ovens for nearly fifty years.

LSDOS started with a strong emphasis on sponsoring Dutch oven cookoffs. However, after holding cookoffs for two years, our membership had increased, and the majority didn't want to cook in competitions, even as Texas friendly as ours. They requested that LSDOS be much more open to gatherings where members could come just to cook a dish or two, have fun, and not have to worry about being judged. A survey was made of our entire membership, and the results were that cookoffs were dropped, and Chapters were formed in the various cities or areas of Texas where they met to hold a "DOG" (Dutch Oven Gathering).

It was further decided that our LSDOS sponsored Chapters would not have any Chapter membership fees nor even a hat passed or any other form of collection of money required to be a Chapter-only member. One could be a Chapter member without also becoming an LSDOS member. Our Chapters hold potluck DOGs where members bring their ovens and cook their favorite dishes for the others to share in eating. There is also an exchange of recipes. We especially like for walk-ins to come visit with us and see, taste, and learn more about the three F's of Dutch oven cooking - Fun, Fellowship, and Food.

Our LSDOS, however, does have a membership fee of $15.00 per year per single person or for a family which includes an issue of our quarterly newsletter, The Dutch Oven. Our newsletter is usually from 18 to as high as 28 pages full of State and Chapter information, tips, upcoming meetings and DOGs, and many pages of recently cooked recipes from all members.

Our doors are always open to anyone, Texan or non-Texan, who wants to join in the fun of Dutch oven cooking. Learn how to cook new and delicious dishes in a Dutch oven on your patio, back yard, or over a campfire.

To join or to find out more about our LSDOS, please contact Bill Brummel, 11434 Castolon Dr., San Antonio, TX 78245-2239, E-Mail: 2bs@stic.net , or Tom Earnest, 5870 Spring Crossing, San Antonio, TX 78247, Email: earnest@swbell.net, or via our LSDOS web site at www.lsdos.com.

PREFACE

In the fall of 1994, the Lone Star Dutch Oven Society was established to form a Texas society for people who were interested in cooking outdoors in Dutch ovens. Societies of Dutch oven cooking have existed in Utah and surrounding states for over ten years. The LSDOS was patterned after the Dutch oven societies in those areas, but we are truly Texas unique. As a result of LSDOS efforts, the Dutch oven is now the official cooking implement of the State of Texas! An important function of LSDOS is to promote the art of Dutch oven cooking.

In 1995 and 1996 the society participated in numerous competitions called Dutch oven cook-offs. At these events the spectators were fascinated by what they saw and eagerly took copies of the recipes that the teams provided. However, there never seemed to be enough copies. The people operating the information booth were bombarded with spectators wanting to know if we had a cookbook. That is how this cookbook came to be. Each of the recipes in this cookbook was prepared in a competition and is tried and true. We sincerely hope that you enjoy the recipes, the history of the recipes, and your Dutch oven.

All of the members of the Lone Star Dutch Oven Society

THE HISTORY OF DUTCH OVENS

(excerpted from an article by Bill Brummel,
1996 & 1997 President of LSDOS)

Cast iron Dutch ovens have been as much a part of the American scene as have colonials, explorers, mountain men, settlers, cattle and sheep men, loggers, gold miners, and Boy Scouts. The black ironware was also extensively used and highly regarded throughout Europe. England was a primary exporter of the cast iron pots, skillets, and kettles through its worldwide fleet. In early America, Dutch traders were said to have traveled from door-to-door selling household goods, including the baking oven, which was supposedly named after the peddlers who sold them. Paul Revere is given the credit as the craftsman who developed the flat-topped Dutch oven with the turned up edge on the lid to hold coals and the three stubby legs on the bottom.

Mountain men favored the simpler and lighter, round-bottomed, no lid, hanging kettle when they were on the move, or maybe even just a skillet. But a Dutch oven was always an essential cooking utensil when they settled into their winter quarters. Wild game stew, beans and biscuits were mighty tasty and warm on the inside when snow was four feet deep and drifting outside! Journals kept by pioneers moving west are sprinkled with references to the Dutch oven. On the lists of necessary utensils for the westward journey of six to eight months, the Dutch oven often led the list followed by "two or three cast iron camp kettles, coffee mill, granite-ware coffee pot, water pail, silverware, tin plate and cups". Everyone was thankful when the train would stop for a day to rest the stock and repair the wagons. On those days the women could cook "light bread" instead of the every day, pan-fried bannock bread. The Dutch oven was the cowboy cook's trusted friend and called for a special place in the chuck wagon in which to travel. Without exception, old photographs and even paintings, by no less than Frederick Remington, show four or five big Dutch ovens around the fire.

Today's Dutch oven is found everywhere the American family is enjoying itself, such as backyard cookouts, family reunions, club and civic get-togethers, Scout camps, church functions, in the mountains and on the rivers. From here to the Pacific, many commercial eateries, dude ranches, outfitters, and river running companies treat their guests to great meals from the black pots. Many of today's Dutch oven cooks were first exposed to the wonderful foods cooked in those black ovens while on a deer hunt or camping trip or most likely with their Scout Troop. Experience has proven that you can cook any recipe, forget a couple of ingredients, even burn it a little bit, and a bunch of hungry Scouts will lap it up, scrape the bottom clean, and then wonder why there wasn't more!

OVERVIEW

The following is adapted from "Outdoor Cooking with Dutch Ovens" by Duane & Sandy Dinwiddie, Texas State Grand Champions in 1995 & 1996.

The most important thing to understand is that cooking with Dutch ovens and charcoal is truly an art, not a science. The same art applies to any cooking with respect to nuances about the recipes and their preparations. The biggest difference between cooking in your kitchen and cooking out of doors is temperature control. In your kitchen, when you set your stove or oven, you can be reasonably sure that the temperatures are going to stay the same. Cooking outdoors with charcoal as your source of heat is very different. The charcoal only burns on the surface, where it can get air. A freshly lit briquette has maybe 4 square inches of surface area, but 30 minutes later might have only 2 square inches. This cuts down the heat produced by a factor of 2. In addition, weather conditions change, with the biggest factor (not counting rain) being wind. Wind affects cooking two ways. First, wind causes the charcoal to burn faster, releasing more heat, but the charcoal doesn't last as long. Second, wind blows heat away from the ovens. The oven will be cooler on the upwind side than on the downwind side, requiring periodic turning of the pot to maintain even heat. In the face of all this, it is still really easy for beginners to learn to cook with a Dutch oven, and is certainly a lot of fun, especially when camping. Except for waffles there is nothing that can't be cooked in one of these ovens.

BUYING AND BREAKING IN AN OVEN

A lot of sporting goods stores now carry Dutch ovens in a range of sizes. A 10 inch oven is a perfect size for two people. A family of four or five should start with a 12-inch oven and Boy Scout leaders should consider buying a 14-inch oven (or two!). The size is the pot diameter in inches and the number is cast into the lid. You will need a charcoal starter also, or you can make one from a 3-pound coffee can with both ends cut out and some holes punched in the sides. You will need something to set the lid on to keep it off the ground (a lid stand) and a tool to pick up the lid when it is loaded with charcoal (lid tool). These items can be purchased or you can make them.

Lone Star Dutch Oven Society Cookbook

The most commonly used ovens are made in Tennessee by a company called Lodge (they also sell accessories). They come with break-in instructions and some recipes. To break in a new oven do the following: The ovens come with a protective material sprayed on them to keep them from rusting during shipment. To get rid of the protective coating, wash the oven with hot water and dishwashing soap. It won't be obvious that you washed anything off, but you did. Thoroughly rinse all the soap out and towel dry. Now the oven must be seasoned. Cast iron is very porous, like a fine sponge. The idea of seasoning is to fill all the fine holes with cooking oil and then convert the oil to carbon with heat. The carbon will eventually fill up all the fine holes and produce a non-stick surface (when oiled just before cooking). The following procedure can be done in your kitchen oven at home, but it will stink up the house due to burning oil. Instead do it outside by setting the oven over about 8 - 10 charcoal briquets and the lid (separately) over the same number, on a lid stand. When they are just too hot to touch with the bare hand, remove from the heat, and thoroughly coat the inside and outside (even the bottom) with solid Crisco® type shortening on a paper towel. It is messy so do it on some newspapers. Then let them cool, and finally wipe the excess shortening out with a paper towel. Heating them up completely dries them and drives out air from the small pores. When coated hot and then allowed to cool, the shortening gets sucked into the pores. Lightly coat the pot inside and out with a good brand of vegetable cooking oil, and bring it up to cooking temperature (about 350°F) for about an hour. Let it cool and wipe out any excess oil with a paper towel and you're ready to cook.

Once the oven has been seasoned, NEVER put soap in it again, or you will un-season it and have to repeat the process. Hot water and a plastic or natural scrub pad will remove anything, even burned material. Never use hard metal utensils as they will scratch the layer of carbon that you are trying to build up inside the oven (soft brass brushes can be used, see later). Store your ovens in a place where they will not be exposed to high humidity or they might rust. Do not oil them for storage, as the oil can get rancid over time (in a hot garage). Oil your Dutch oven with a light vegetable cooking oil just before use, inside and out, and the protective carbon coating on the pot will build up over time. If you can smell rancid oil in a pot after prolonged storage you must clean it out. Normal use will gradually build up a thickened oil coating that feels waxy and is brown to black in color. This is the good stuff. It is unthickened oil that goes rancid. To clean out a pot to remove rancid oil smells, warm the pot up and pour in a liberal amount of cooking oil. Then scrub for about 5 minutes and the rancid layer should dissolve off. Discard the scrubbing oil and wipe the pot clean with a paper towel. If thè pot still smells rancid, then you must burn it out. Simply put a full layer of charcoal under the pot and a full layer of charcoal on the lid, with the charcoal briquets laying flat and just touching each other. After about 5 minutes, quickly wipe out the inside of the pot with a wad of paper towels to remove as much of the oil as you can. Try to do this with the pot very hot. After that, lift the lid every 10 to 20 minutes to let the smoke out. Burn it until only a small amount of smoke comes out of the pot when you lift the lid (for large pots, about an hour). You are converting the waxy oils to carbon deposits in addition to removing rancid oils. If you don't wipe out the excess oil at first when the pot first gets hot, loose carbon will be formed like scale in the pot, and it must be removed (use a soft brass brush). The pot is still seasoned after properly burning it out so just oil it before cooking and you are in business. With a new pot, try to avoid cooking things with a lot of water or acids (tomatoes) in the pot at first, as they will tend to get into the unfilled pores and try to rust the pot. Stick with frying or baking for the first few tries and then you'll be okay. Pinto beans are also very damaging to a pot's seasoning.

TIDBITS

Beginners frequently over-start their charcoal. By that I mean, they leave it in the starter too long before they use it. It should take only 10 to 15 minutes to start charcoal in a chimney starter and anything longer than that is a waste. It may not look lit in the starter but if it has flames coming out the top and no smoke, it is ready. Charcoal that has been started for 30 minutes before it is put on the pot will be half burned away and will not produce as much heat per briquet. It will also not provide heat long enough to finish some recipes. Always start more charcoal than you need so you can add the extra later to maintain heat if necessary, especially if it is windy.

CHARCOAL

"THE DINWIDDIE METHOD OF CHARCOAL BRIQUET USE"

Throughout this book there is reference to 'The Dinwiddie Method of Charcoal Briquet Use'. It is as follows:

> Counting the number of charcoal briquets used under and on top of an oven can be misleading, since the temperature will vary based on the size of the lit charcoal. Charcoal that has been lit for a while is smaller and won't put out as much heat. The following geometric patterns correct this, as you have to use more small briquets to make a complete ring than larger ones, which automatically adjusts the number you put on the pot.
>
> 1 ring: If you make a circle of hot charcoal with all of the briquets lying flat and touching each other (with spaces left out for the legs on the bottom rings), that is "one ring".
>
> 1/2-ring: A "half-ring" is the same size circle, but with every other briquet missing.
>
> 2 rings: Add a second ring inside the "1 ring", touching each other.
>
> full spread: means to put all the briquets you can (one layer deep laying flat) either under, very rare, (except in frying) or on top of the pot.
>
> **All rings start with the outside edge of the briquets lined up with the outside edge of the oven. . . . . top or bottom.** You will rapidly learn about how many charcoal briquets it takes to make rings for different size ovens and what the corresponding cooking temperatures are.

Temperature Control

It is possible to cook almost everything there is to cook with just four temperatures.....slow, medium, hot and very hot. Using 'The Dinwiddie Method of Charcoal Briquet Use' for a 10 inch oven, slow will have 1 ring on top, and 1 loose ring under the pot and be 300°F +/- 25 degrees. Medium is 1-ring under and 1½ rings on top and is 350°F +/- 25 degrees. A hot oven is 1 ring under and 2 rings on top and is 400°F +/- 25 degrees, and very hot is 1-ring under and 2½ rings on top and is 450°F or so. For larger pots, you will need more charcoal on top for each temperature. For example, two rings on top of a 10 inch pot covers half the lid surface but only 1/4 of the lid surface area on a 14 inch pot. You will quickly learn to adjust the absolute amount of charcoal for different size pots. For frying, start with a full spread under the pot and fry with the lid on to keep the heat in. Whatever you are cooking, look inside the pot periodically to see if your food is simmering properly, or browning properly, etc., and add or take away charcoal as needed. Start a personal cookbook or jot notes in the spaces provided thorough out this cookbook including how much charcoal you used, how long you cooked it and whether it was done correctly. It is best to err on the hot side as it is really hard to burn something in these pots. The final answer is to practice and keep records. You will rapidly learn how much charcoal it takes to make your pot do what you want it to.

MORE INFORMATION
ABOUT COOKING IN THE DUTCH OVEN

The following information was adapted from the Lodge Manufacturing Company's pamphlet called 'Lodge Dutch Ovens... "100 years & Still Cooking" written by Bill Brummel, an LSDOS founding member. We wanted to include this information since many Dutch oven cookbooks are silent on the subject.

After seasoning your oven, the first step to get cooking is to start up some hot coals or briquets to cook with! If using wood, get the fire going 30 - 45 minutes before needing coals. If using briquets, ignite them about 15 - 20 minutes before you need them. As the coals are getting hot, prepare your ingredients and ovens for cooking, use a good brand of charcoal briquets as you can better control the amount of heat inside your oven. Arrange the number of briquets needed by placing them under the oven's bottom in a circular pattern so they are at least 1/2" inside the oven's edge. Arrange the briquets on top of the lid in a checkerboard pattern. Top or bottom, do not bunch the briquets as that can cause "hot spot" problems in cooking, lift and rotate the oven 1/4 turn every 10 - 15 minutes and then rotate the lid 1/4 turn in the opposite direction. Check your foods occasionally to make sure they're not burning, cooking too fast, or not cooking fast enough. Be careful in removing the lids so as not to flavor your dish with ashes! If necessary to add or remove briquets, do so in the same proportions top and bottom. Keep food warm after cooking by removing all briquets except for a few both under and over the oven. With practice, you'll become better at controlling your cooking temperatures. This is part of the fun and challenge of cooking with Dutch ovens! However, you can use the following chart as an aid in getting started. The figure to the right of the oven sizes is the total number of briquets required, and the figures directly below those are the number of top/bottom briquets required to attain the temperature stated at the top of the chart.

BAKING TEMPERATURE CHART

OVEN	TEMPERATURE REQUIRED					
	325°F	350°F	375°F	400°F	425°F	450°F
8"	15	16	17	18	19	20
	10/5	11/5	11/6	12/6	13/6	14/6
10"	19	21	23	25	27	29
	13/6	14/7	16/7	17/8	18/9	19/10
12"	23	25	27	29	31	33
	16/7	17/8	18/9	19/10	21/10	22/11
14"	30	32	34	36	38	40
	22/12	24/12	22/12	24/12	25/13	26/14
16"	34	36	38	40	42	44
	22/12	24/12	25/13	27/13	28/14	30/14

Baking temperatures taken from regular cookbooks, sometimes refer to Slow, Moderate, Hot, or Very Hot ovens. Those terms normally reflect the average following F degrees.
    Slow - 250°F - 350°F, Moderate - 350°F - 400°F, Hot - 400°F - 450°F, Very Hot - 450°F - 500°F.

Through this book, individual recipes call for widely varying amounts of charcoal to get the same cooking temperatures. This just shows how much room there is for true temperature differences without ruining the food in a Dutch oven.

Notes

ACKNOWLEDGMENTS

I would like to thank the following people for helping make this cookbook a reality. I first would like to thank Sandy Dinwiddie for all her help with editing and proofing the recipes in this book. Her assistance and suggestions have helped keep the recipes consistent and clear. I want to thank Duane Dinwiddie for his graphics that appear in a number of places in the pages of the book and for sharing with us the introductory pages of his Dutch oven cooking class booklet. I want to thank Bill Brummel for the ad that has helped pay for some of the printing and for generously allowing us to use the information he supplied to the Lodge Manufacturing Company for their pamphlet "100 Years and Still Cooking." Most of all I want to thank all of those who participated in the cook-offs held throughout Texas during 1995 and 1996. Thank you for sharing your recipes but most of all thank you for sharing the stories behind those recipes. It's the *Historical Notes* included with so many of the recipes that makes this a true Texas treasury of Dutch oven cooking.

- Nancy P. Alemany

Breakfast

Breakfast Turkey and Cream Gravy

12 inch Dutch oven - Feeds 8 to 10 people

2 - 3 pounds of turkey breast, cut into strips
some flour
salt & pepper to taste
warm water

Cut the breast into strips. Season the strips with salt and pepper, then dust with flour. Get your Dutch oven good and hot, add a small amount of oil and brown the turkey strips until they are about 3/4 ths done.

Remove the turkey from the Dutch oven and wipe the oven clean. Place oven back on the coals and add enough water to fill the oven about half full. Add flour a little bit at a time, whisking it until it is smooth. Gravy should be thin and runny but should have a good color and texture when you have added enough flour.

Place browned turkey back in pot and cover. Simmer for about 1 hour. Check regularly to make sure gravy is not too thick. If gravy gets too thick just add some more hot water to thin it back down. Gravy should be thin when serving. Check to see if it has enough spice, if not, add more salt and pepper.

Serve warm over fresh, home made biscuits.

Historical Note:

This is an old family recipe that my great grandfather cooked in camp. My grandfather was famous for this dish in deer camps across the state. My father continues to cook this dish in deer camps. There are no set rules or measurements because at hunting camp you never know how much you need to make, or how much you have to make it with. You can spice it up and make a lunch out of it or it is just as good for supper.

- The Hatfield Ranch Cocineros
Dan Hatfield & Cindy Rather
Medina, TX

Hash Brown Quiche

12 inch Dutch oven - Serves 6 hungry campers - 8 regular people

5 cups shredded potatoes for hash browns
1 tomato
1 2/3 cups diced fully cooked ham or link sausage
1 2/3 cups shredded Cheddar cheese
¾ cup milk
½ cup butter, melted
5 eggs
½ cup onions, diced
1 small can parmesan cheese
½ tsp salt
1 - 4 oz can mushrooms, sliced
2 Tbsp Worcestershire sauce

Preheat Dutch oven with 18 briquets under the bottom, or cook on the inverted lid. Add 2 Tbsp butter, onions, mushrooms, ham or sausage and Worcestershire sauce. Sauté until onions become transparent, then remove from Dutch oven and set aside. Let oven cool, wipe clean.

Press hashed potatoes between towels to remove excess moisture. Press hashed potatoes into the bottom and up the sides of the Dutch oven about 1 inch. Drizzle 1/3 cup butter on potatoes.

Set up Dutch oven to bake at 425°F for 25 minutes. **(21 briquets on top, 10 on the bottom)** After 25 minutes set up Dutch oven to bake at 350°F, **(17 briquets on top, 8 on the bottom)**

Spoon onions, mushrooms, and sausage mix over hash brown potato crust. Spread shredded Cheddar cheese over all.

In a small bowl beat eggs, milk, salt and pepper. Pour over all in the Dutch oven.
Bake for 25 minutes.

- The Chuckle Wagon Cookers
Steve & Jeanice Bias
La Marque, TX

Scrambled Eggs Ranchero
14 inch Dutch oven - 12 Servings

RANCHERO SAUCE:
4 ½ cups canned plum tomatoes, chopped
¼ cup vegetable oil
½ cup onion, chopped   ½ tsp sugar
1 clove garlic, minced   1 tsp salt
½ tsp oregano   ½ tsp pepper
½ tsp basil   ½ tsp cumin

Preheat Dutch oven with 18 briquets under the bottom. Sauté onion and garlic in hot oil for 5 minutes or until lightly golden. Add tomatoes and spices. Simmer for 30 minutes. Stir occasionally to avoid scorching. Remove to a bowl and wipe oven clean.

WHITE SAUCE:
3 Tbsp butter   1 cup milk
2 Tbsp flour   salt & pepper to taste

Melt butter and blend in flour to make a roux. Cook slowly for two minutes without browning. Add milk slowly. Stir until smooth. Simmer 5 minutes. Remove to a bowl and wipe oven clean.

EGGS:
    12 eggs lightly beaten
    2 Tbsp butter
    1 -.4 oz can chopped mild chilies

Melt butter, add eggs and chilies and stir constantly. Keep eggs on soft side, remove from heat, add white sauce. Mix well. Set aside.

ASSEMBLY:
    12 corn tortillas
    12 thin slices cooked ham
    4 oz mild Cheddar cheese, grated
    3 jalapeno peppers, sliced
    6 sprigs fresh cilantro, chopped

Place a slice of ham on each tortilla. Place some scrambled eggs on ham. Shape into a roll. Cover bottom of 14 inch Dutch oven with part of ranchero sauce. Place tortilla rolls in Dutch oven. Cover with remaining ranchero sauce. Sprinkle with grated cheese. Scatter sliced jalapeno peppers on top. Cover and cook at 350°F for 15 minutes until tortillas are soft and cheese is melted. Garnish with fresh cilantro just before serving.

- Ike Craddock & Bill Spangler
Medina, TX

Sausage and Gravy

14 inch Dutch oven

1 lb sausage
½ cup flour
5 cups milk
2 Tbsp Pace® Hot Picanté Salsa

Preheat Dutch oven with 18 briquets on the bottom.

Fry meat till browned. Remove meat from Dutch oven. Drain off all fat except about ¼ cup. Add flour, stirring constantly until browned. Add milk and cook until thickened. Add the cooked sausage and the salsa to the gravy. Stir well and serve over biscuits or toast.

- Beverly Modgling
Medina, TX

Huevos de Monterey

12 inch Dutch oven - Serves 10 - 12

12 eggs
1 cup milk
2 tsp salt
1 tsp pepper
4 - 5 medium jalapenos
2 cups Monterey Jack cheese, shredded
8 slices white bread

6 slices bacon
1 medium onion, chopped
6 medium mushrooms, sliced small
6 Tbsp butter/margarine

Combine eggs, milk, salt and pepper in a bowl, beating well. Add jalapenos and cheese, mix well.

Preheat Dutch oven - with 18 briquets on the bottom.

Fry bacon crisp in Dutch oven. Set aside bacon and crumble into small pieces. Sauté onions and mushrooms in bacon fat until onions are transparent. Add to egg mixture. Pour out most of the bacon fat. Spread butter over one side of each bread slice, cut each slice into 4 triangles. Arrange ½ of the bread triangles, butter side out and cut side down, around the edge of the oven. Arrange remaining bread slices, buttered side down, in bottom of the Dutch oven. Pour egg mixture, SLOWLY, over bread slices.

Bake at 350°F **(Start with 10 coals under the Dutch oven and 14 - 16 coals on the lid)** for ½ hour until egg is set. Test with knife inserted in center. If bread crust around edge is not crunchy, add more coals on top during the last 10 minutes of cooking.

Historical Note:

Years ago while vacationing in Mexico, we took a long horseback ride to a hidden ranch where we stayed awhile. There were about 20 vaqueros having lunch under a huge spreading oak tree, and were invited to join them. This recipe approximates the meal we were given.

- Bungy Hartshorn
Bandera, TX

Sausage Omelet

14 inch Dutch oven - 15 Servings

3 packages sausage pork links
¼ cup onion, minced
¼ cup green pepper, sliced
15 large eggs
¼ cup milk
3 medium tomatoes, chopped
4 Tbsp butter

Heat sausage in Dutch oven until brown. Remove links and keep warm. Sauté onion and green pepper in Dutch oven over 20 coals until vegetables are tender. Combine eggs and milk in a bowl, add to this the onion, green pepper, and tomato. Melt butter in Dutch oven over 10 coals. Add egg mixture and cook until almost set. Arrange sausage on top of eggs. To finish cooking the omelet, put as many coals as you can on lid and cook until lightly browned.

- Paul & Sissy Garrison
Medina, TX

Hunter's Hashbrown Breakfast Pie

12 inch Dutch oven - Serves 8 - 10

(NOTE: Underlined ingredients are TEXAS grown & produced!)

½ lb venison sausage, cut into small pieces
1 medium chopped onion
2 - 3 lbs raw grated potatoes, squeezed dry or 20 - 30 oz pre-
    packaged "hash brown potatoes"
12 eggs
2 cups grated Monterey Jack cheese
1 - 8-oz jar hot, medium or mild Pace® Picanté Sauce

Hunter's Hashbrown Breakfast Pie continued. . . . .

Hunter's Hashbrown Breakfast Pie continued. . . . .
Preheat Dutch oven with 20 - 25 coals, bottom only. Brown ½ lb venison sausage. Add 1 medium chopped onion and cook until translucent. Remove sausage and onions from Dutch oven and drain on paper towels, keeping the cooked ingredients warm by placing them on the lid over 5 - 6 coals until ready to add back into pot.

Wipe excess grease out of Dutch oven and place back over hot coals. Stir in hash brown potatoes. Fry until potatoes are golden brown, then mix the sausage and onions back in. Reduce bottom heat to 10 coals.

Break 12 eggs into medium mixing bowl and beat thoroughly. Pour over potatoes, sausage and onions. Cover with hot lid (14 coals on top) and cook until eggs are almost solid. Sprinkle with grated cheese. Continue cooking until eggs set and cheese melts. Just before serving, top with Picanté sauce to taste

Historical Note:
This recipe came with our newest Lodge Dutch oven. Instead of bacon, we used venison sausage made from Hill Country white-tail deer! In addition, we felt we needed a hotter fire to start with than their recipe called for.

- Mark & Pennie Prislovsky,
Kerrville, TX

The Two B's Texas Hill Country Breakfast

12 inch Dutch oven - Serves 8 - 10

1 lb lite pork sausage
1 medium onion, diced
2 lbs baking potatoes, peeled and shredded
8 large eggs
½ lb Cheddar cheese, grated
½ lb Monterey Jack cheese, grated
1-8 oz jar Pace® Thick & Chunky Salsa

Breakfast

Preheat oven with 14 briquets under pot. Brown sausage, breaking it into small bits. Add onion and cook until onion is translucent (clear). Remove sausage and onions, drain on paper towels. Wipe out excess grease from oven and place back over coals. Stir in shredded potatoes and fry until golden brown. Add sausage and onions back and mix thoroughly.

Remove 4 briquets from bottom and add to lid. Add 12 fresh briquets to the top.

Break eggs into mixing bowl and beat thoroughly. Pour eggs over mixture in oven, cover with lid and cook until eggs are almost solid. Sprinkle cheese over mixture and continue cooking until eggs set and cheese melts. Just before serving, top with salsa.
Serve warm and enjoy!

Historical Note:
This recipe is a modification of a recipe supplied by Lodge Manufacturing Co. that comes with the new Dutch ovens. We've adapted it to be more 'heart healthful' than the original recipe. You can adjust the salsa's heat according to your preference. However, beware that the sausage also carries a nice amount of seasoning and you may not want to override it's flavor.

- The Two B's Dutch Oven Team
Bill & Beverly Brummel
San Antonio, TX

Notes

Beef

Arkansas Beef Casserole

14 inch Dutch oven

2½ lbs ground beef
4 Tbsp butter or margarine
1 tsp garlic juice
2 small cans tomato sauce
1½ tsp salt
½ tsp pepper
1 tsp sugar

8 oz cream cheese
16 oz sour cream
4 green onions (tops and all)
10 oz medium egg noodles
1 cup Cheddar cheese grated
2 cans cream of mushroom soup

Brown meat in butter. Add garlic juice and simmer 20 minutes. Add tomato sauce, salt, pepper, and sugar. Simmer 15 minutes more. In a separate bowl mix cream cheese, sour cream, and chopped onions; set aside. Cook noodles as directed on package. Layer noodles, meat, grated cheese and sour cream mixture in a 14 inch Dutch oven. Top casserole with undiluted mushroom soup and garnish as desired. Bake in a moderate oven or 350°F. To obtain the desired oven temperature of 350°F use 11 coals under the oven and 17 coals on top.

- Jimma & Shannon Morris
Austin, Arkansas

Beef and Beans

14 inch Dutch oven

¼ lb bacon
3 lbs ground beef
½ small onion, diced
3 medium potatoes, diced

3 - 4 mushrooms, diced
2 - 31 oz cans pork and beans
1 cup molasses
½ cup ketchup

16 - 20 charcoal briquets to start.

Place 16 - 20 briquets under 14 inch Dutch oven and fry bacon until crisp. Remove bacon and drain on paper towel. Wipe grease out of

Beef

oven. Brown ground beef with onion and potato. Drain off excess grease and add beans, ketchup, molasses and mushrooms. Crumble bacon and add to mixture. Cover and adjust heat to 12 briquets below and 16 briquets on top. Simmer, stirring occasionally until mushrooms are tender and mixture is thoroughly blended, about 30 minutes.

- Scott & Debbie Ragland
Duncanville, TX

Beef Bourguignon
12 inch Dutch oven

4 slices bacon, diced ½ inch	2 cloves garlic, minced
1 - 10½ oz can beef stock	2 - 3 cups dry red wine
1 Tbsp tomato paste	8 small pearl onions
½ tsp leaf thyme	½ lb fresh mushrooms, sliced
1 tsp salt, or to taste	butter
freshly ground black pepper	1 bay leaf
minced parsley	cooking oil

3 lbs lean boneless beef, cut in 1 inch cubes (as tender as your purse permits)

Place a 12 inch Dutch oven over 20 briquets. Fry the bacon bits until crisp. Remove bacon and set aside. Add a little oil to the bacon grease. Use tongs and begin to brown the meat. Use care and do not add too much meat to the pot at one time. As the meat is browned on all sides, remove the pieces and set aside. When all the meat has been browned and removed. Deglaze the oven by adding 2 cups of the red wine. Scrape the bottom to remove any bits that may be stuck.

Now add one half of the beef bouillon, tomato paste, thyme, salt, pepper, bay leaf, and garlic. Return the browned meat to the oven. As soon as this mixture has started to simmer remove all but 7
Beef Bourguignon continued. . . . .

Beef Bourguignon continued.....
briquets under the pot. Cover and let this cool. Meanwhile, in another pot, sauté the sliced mushrooms in a little butter until they are almost done. Also, in another pot, par-boil the pearl onions in the rest of the beef bouillon and a little water for about 15 minutes. When the meat is done, make a paste by creaming 1 Tbsp butter with 1 ½ Tbsp flour. Incorporate a little of the hot pan juices into this until it is well mixed. Then add this to the pot, stirring constantly until the gravy is thickened. Add mushrooms and onions to the pot. Cover and simmer so that the flavors combine.

Beef Bourguignon may also be served with cooked rice, a green salad, a good wine and French bread.

Historical Note
This recipe is from *Southern Living Party Cookbook, Complete Menus & Entertaining Guide*, by Celia Marks. 1972 edition, pp. 185-186. Adapted to the Dutch oven by Los Dos Compadres.

- Los Dos Compadres
Wayne Adam & Gary Grogan
Wharton, TX

Beef in the Garden

12 inch Dutch oven - Serves 10 - 12

2 lbs lean chuck, cut into 1 inch cubes
3 Tbsp all purpose flour
2 large onions, cut into ¾ inch pieces
4 cloves garlic, coarsely chopped
1 cup mushrooms, coarsely chopped
2 jalapenos, stemmed, seeded, chopped
3 - 4 Tbsp olive oil
6 potatoes, scrubbed and de-eyed, ¼ inch slices with skins on
3 bell peppers, without seeds & membranes, sliced
6 - 8 carrots, peeled, sliced into 1/8th inch thick diagonals
1 - 16 oz can whole, peeled tomatoes, with liquid

Beef

1 - 15¼ oz can sweet peas, with liquid
1 - 15¼ oz can whole kernel sweet corn, with liquid
6 stalks celery, washed, with tops, sliced diagonally
1 bunch broccoli, washed, large stems removed, florets separated
salt & coarse ground pepper, to taste
2 bay leaves, whole
1 tsp each of cilantro leaves & rosemary leaves
2 Tbsp corn starch
2 Tbsp cold water

Heat oven with oil until water droplets sizzle. Add beef pieces after coating with flour, sauté until all sides are browned to seal in meat juices. Set meat aside. Add more oil as necessary, sauté onions, and garlic until just transparent, add mushrooms and jalapenos. Stir well to finish the sauté. Reduce heat to 375°F - 400°F. Add cut potato pieces, sliced bell peppers, carrots, meat, tomato, corn and peas all with liquid. Add bay leaves, salt, pepper, cilantro and rosemary. Stir well. With lid in place, cook until potatoes are done (stick with a fork). When all is tender, meat included, add broccoli by laying it on top to steam for 10 minutes. Remove bay leaves and any excess liquid. Mix corn starch with cold water and mix well into remaining liquid in pot. Continue heating for another couple minutes until liquid thickens. Serve while hot.

Historical Note

Background: - There is none!!! Plain ole beef stew has been around since man learned to grunt. The only changes are the gozinta which varies with what is displayed at the store. Yes, great grand-mother made this as well.

- Larry Hartshorn
Bandera, TX

Big Bend Beefy Bell Peppers

14 inch Dutch oven - Serves 8

2 lbs lean ground beef
8 medium bell peppers
2 cups onions, chopped Mix
8 oz tomato soup
32 oz V-8® type juice

2 cups crushed saltine crackers
2 eggs
2 pkgs. Lipton® Onion Soup
2 Tbsp parsley
salt & pepper, to taste

Brown ground beef with all dry ingredients in 14 inch medium hot Dutch oven (18 to 20 coals on bottom) drain off fat then add soup and eggs and cook well. Remove meat mixture and set aside.

Prepare bell peppers by filling with meat mixture. Arrange prepared bell peppers inside the Dutch oven. Cover bell peppers approximately 1/2 way up sides of bell pepper with V-8® type juice.

Cover Dutch oven and cook with medium hot heat 18 - 20 coals (2/3 on top, 1/3 on bottom) for 45 minutes. Garnish with grated Colby cheese and parsley. Enjoy

- Wayne & Jay Switzer
Fort Worth, TX

Biscuit Casserole

12 inch Dutch oven - Serves 8

2½ lbs ground chuck or sirloin
1 onion, chopped
½ bell pepper, chopped
1 can Fiesta® Tomato soup
½ cup catsup
salt & pepper, to taste
American cheese slices or grated Cheddar cheese
Prepared biscuits - may be homemade, made from a mix or canned.

Sauté meat in 12 inch Dutch oven with onion and bell pepper. Lightly salt and pepper. Add tomato soup and catsup. Arrange sliced cheese or grated cheese on meat mixture then cover entirely with biscuits. Bake at 375°F (with 8 coals on bottom and 12 coals on top) until biscuits are golden brown.

- Shem & Norma Ray
Sulphur Springs, TX

Bitter Creek Bake

12 inch Dutch oven - Feeds 6 hongry outlaws!

BILL OF MATERIALS:
1½ lbs good ground beef
1½ tsp ground cumin
1 Tbsp chili powder
¼ tsp cayenne pepper
1 tsp black pepper
1 tsp salt or to taste
1/8 tsp allspice
1 rounded tsp chopped garlic
2 - 10 oz cans diced tomatoes & green chilies
  (Rotel® or equivalent) juice and all
12 corn tortillas
1 lb farmers cheese (or ricotta or drained small curd cottage cheese)
¼ cup tequila (optional, but it burns up)
1 cup grated Monterey Jack cheese
1 chopped jalapeno pepper, cleaned of seeds and membrane
1 egg

GARNISH:
½ cup grated Cheddar cheese
2 cups shredded lettuce
½ cup chopped tomatoes
3 green onions, chopped
Bitter Creek Bake continued . . . . .

Lone Star Dutch Oven Society Cookbook

Bitter Creek Bake continued . . . . .
¼ cup sliced black olives
1 Tbsp chopped cilantro, if desired

ASSEMBLY INSTRUCTIONS:
- Start 25 or so charcoal briquets.
- Brown ground beef in a 12 inch oven. Drain cooked beef and pour into a mixing container. Stir spices and the tomatoes into the beef.
- Cover bottom and about 2 inches up side of oven with about 7 of the tortillas. Pour beef mixture over tortillas on the bottom. Place about 5 tortillas on top of the beef and set the oven a side.
- In same mixing container, mix ricotta cheese, shredded Monterey Jack cheese, egg and tequila; pour over tortillas in the oven. Put lid on with 10 coals on bottom, 10 - 15 on top and bake for about 30 minutes. After 15 min., watch coals on bottom so dish won't burn.
- While the dish cooks, prepare garnish. The dish is done when the cheese mixture sets and is bubbly. Remove from heat and arrange garnish in rows or other attractive pattern on top of the cooked food in the oven. Present the dish. ***ENJOY!***

Historical Note

This recipe was given to me by Mr. Hickman, a sourdough hunter, trapper and gold pannier who had a gold claim up in Bitter Creek Canyon north of Red River, NM. I used to stay in his cabin while trout fishing on Bitter Creek back in the 50's and 60's. Hickman used to tell tall tales around the campfire, especially if you could supply some "cough medicine". Hickman said that he made a living during WW2 by hauling scrap iron from the old mines and selling it for the war effort. Sadly, he and the place are gone now,.

  - From the *OutLaw Gazette*
  Hole in the Wall Press
  Sulphur Springs, TX
  Capt. Joe Scott, editor

Blue Plate Special

12 inch Dutch oven - Serves 4

1 lb round steak, ¼ inch thick	1 tsp salt
1 cup flour	1 cup bacon dripping
1 large onion	or lard
2 - 15 oz can peeled tomatoes (chopped)	1 small bell pepper
3 Tbsp Worcestershire sauce	3 Tbsp brown sugar
3 Tbsp chili powder	1 Tbsp vinegar
salt & pepper (see instructions)	

Cut steak into 6 or more pieces. Pound the putty out of each piece to tenderize then salt, pepper and flour each piece. Over 10 coals, brown in about 4 Tbsp of bacon grease. Set aside on oven lid. Slice onion and bell pepper very thin, add to pot and brown. Dust some flour into the pot to brown also. Add tomatoes and other ingredients. Put steak into pot and mix well. The Blue Plate special now cooks best with most heat on top - 15 coals or so on the top and 8 on the bottom. About 1 hour or more works well. Before serving check for enough salt.

Historical Note

My mother served this for as long as I can remember. It was not a special dish at our house - Chicken on Sunday was - but it was my favorite. It was my grandmother's recipe. I'm sure it came from the cabins because Nettie would always cook it at Grandmother's house. Now, without saying too much, which really isn't my style, I'll just tell you, I'm not talking yesterday. Anyway, Mother taught me and I taught my wife, and then it got converted to the black pot. Now I'm teaching my grandson.

- Joe Williamson
Sulphur Springs, TX

Carne De Campo
(Camp Beef)
14 inch Dutch oven - Serves 6 - 8

3 lbs beef loin
5 medium potatoes
5 medium carrots
5 small onions
2 tsp pepper
2 tsp salt
½ tsp garlic powder
1 Tbsp oil

For garnish:
    mushrooms
    bell peppers
    or Cilantro

Place oven over 8 briquets. Cut up 2 onions and place in oven with 1 Tbsp oil. Rub beef loin with salt, pepper and garlic, then place on top of onions and cover lid. Add 8 briquets to lid. Cook 40 - 60 minutes, then add "Big Cut" potatoes and carrots with ¾ cup water. Replace lid and cook for 1 hour. Keep lid hot with fresh coals. During last 10 minutes of cooking garnish with mushrooms and a few cuts of bell pepper.

- Cooking Team of Ed Rehfeld & Jim Clark
Corpus Christi, TX

Tin Plate Special
12 inch Dutch oven

1 lb round steak
oil - just to cover bottom
flour
salt & pepper
1 tsp onion powder
1 cup beef stock or water

Steak should be cut thin, about ¼ inch thick. Cut into 6 pieces.

Beef

Pound to make tender. Then salt, pepper and flour each piece. Brown quickly in oil over hot fire. Remove meat to pot lid. Now add about 6 Tbsp of oil and about 4 Tbsp of flour and make a dark brown roux. To this mixture add the stock or water and onion powder. Return the meat to the pot and cover. Cook until tender, about 325°F. More stock may need to be added during cooking. Gravy should be medium thickness.

When browning the meat, 15 briquets or more should be used to insure a hot fire. Once browning is completed, then only 7 briquets on the bottom and about 10 on top.

- Joe & Ann Williamson
Sulphur Springs, TX

Dutch Oven Pot Roast

12 inch Dutch oven - Serves 4 - 6

4 - 5 lbs shoulder roast
1 lb potatoes
1 large onion
3 - 4 large carrots
salt, pepper, garlic and bay leaves to taste
butter, oil or shortening to taste
2 - 4 cups water

Heat oven over coals using a **full spread***. Rub meat with salt, pepper and crushed garlic. Brown lightly in butter, oil or shortening. Add 2 cups boiling water and chopped vegetables. Remove some of coals so there's **1 ring*** on the bottom and **1 ½ rings*** on the top. Cover oven with lid and place coals on lid. Check periodically to add water if necessary. Cook 2 hours. Replace coals as needed.

Historical Note
This is one of the easiest things to cook in a Dutch oven.

*See 'Dinwiddie Method of Charcoal Briquet Use' on page 10.

Old Fashioned Pot Roast

14 inch Dutch oven - Serves 6 (or four deer hunters)

1 - 3 to 5 lbs chuck roast
2 - 10 oz cans of cream of mushroom soup
6 - 8 large, russet potatoes (quartered)
1 lb carrots (chunk sliced)
1 pkg. Lipton® onion soup mix
1 tsp black pepper
1 pinch of salt

Preheat 14 inch Dutch oven with 10 - 12 coals on the bottom of the oven. Place the onions in the hot oven until clear, then set aside. Pepper the roast evenly on both sides and lightly brown the roast for about 3 - 5 minutes. Then place the clarified onions on the browned roast. Add the remaining ingredients and blend evenly. Cook for about one hour in a medium hot Dutch oven.

Instructions for medium hot Dutch oven (350°F):
25 charcoal briquets - place 2/3 of coals on top of Dutch oven and 1/3 coals on the bottom of the Dutch oven.

- Alan & Wayne Switzer
Fort Worth, TX

Rancher's Meat Pie

'A Taste of Old West Texas Ranch Cooking'
12 inch Dutch oven - Serves 12

2 lbs beef, (chuck) cut into ¾ inch cubes
2 cups onions (2 large), chopped
6 potatoes, medium size, peeled, cubed
4 carrots, medium, peeled, quartered and cut into 1 inch long pieces
2 jalapenos, minced
½ cup mushrooms, sliced, dried or fresh
2 - 10 oz cans Rotel® tomato-pepper sauce, drained

Beef

1 - 8 oz can tomato sauce
4 medium sized sweet green peppers, chopped
2 cups canned whole kernel corn, drained
2 Tbsp chili powder
3 tsp salt
2 tsp pepper

Brown beef until no longer pink and onions are translucent in an oiled 12 inch pot. Stir in potatoes, carrots, jalapenos, mushrooms, Rotel® tomato-pepper sauce, green peppers, corn, chili powder, salt, and pepper. Bring to a boil, lower heat, cover and simmer 15 minutes. Use 12 briquets under and 16 over.

Crust: *(a cumin-pecan corn bread)*

2 cups all-purpose flour	2 tsp baking powder
1½ cups yellow corn meal	½ tsp salt
4 Tbsp sugar	½ tsp cayenne pepper (*)
3 tsp cumin seed (*)	2 cups milk
½ cup vegetable or olive oil	2 large eggs
1 large red bell pepper, chopped(*)	1 1/3 cups chopped pecans (*)

Note: For quick prep., use 2 pkgs. ready mix cornbread mix. Mix per package directions and add items with (*) above.

Mix dry ingredients in a large bowl. Whisk milk, oil, and egg in a small bowl to blend. Add milk mixture to dry ingredients and stir just until evenly moistened. Mix in red bell pepper and pecans. Pour batter on top of meat mixture. Bake at 400°F (6 briquets under and 20 briquets on top) until top is a golden brown and tester inserted into center comes out clean, about 30 - 35 minutes.

Historical Note

The idea for this recipe is from Stella Hughes book *Bacon & Beans, Ranch-Country Recipes.* Highly modified, more vegetables and spice added for a heartier and tastier treat and a completely different crust for a distinctive flavor variation

- Larry & Bungy Hartshorn,
Bandera, TX

Sassy Meat Loaf Ring

12 inch Dutch oven - serves 10 - 12 Hungry Folks

MEAT LOAF:
2 eggs, beaten
¼ cup Carnation® nonfat dry milk
½ cup Old London's® fine, unseasoned dry bread crumbs
¼ cup onion, finely chopped
2 Tbsp Heart-Loc's® Parsley Flakes
1 tsp Morton® Salt
1 tsp Adams'® Ground Sage
½ tsp McCormick® Garlic Salt
½ cup Pace® Thick and Chunky Salsa (We used extra mild.)
2 lbs H-E-B®'s 80 - 85 % Lean Ground Beef
GLAZE:
¼ cup H-E-B®'S 'Easy Squeezy' catsup
2 Tbsp Imperial® brown sugar
1¼ tsp McCormick® dry mustard
½ tsp Realemon® concentrated lemon juice

- In a bowl, combine the eggs and milk. Stir in the bread crumbs, onion, parsley, salt, sage, pepper, and garlic salt. Add ground beef. Thoroughly mix everything.
- Spoon the meat mixture into a 5½ cups ring mold and firmly pat it down. Carefully unmold the meat mixture into the Dutch oven.
- Using Kingsford® charcoal, set up the Dutch oven to cook with 9 briquets under the bottom. Cover and bake for 50 minutes with 14 briquets of top of lid. If necessary, use turkey baster or spoon to remove excess meat drippings.
- Glaze the meat by combining the catsup, brown sugar, dry mustard, and lemon juice. Carefully remove the oven cover and spread the sauce mixture over the meat loaf. Replace the cover and bake for an additional 10 - 15 minutes. You may have to add fresh briquets, 4 - 5 to bottom and 7 - 8 on top, to finish cooking.
- Fill the center ring of meat loaf with vegetables or mashed potatoes, garnish as you desire. We use mashed potatoes garnished with carrots, parsley and red and green peppers julienned. Serve and Enjoy!

Beef

Historical Note

We've modified a recipe found in *Dutch Oven Cooking with Tony Cano* by Tony Cano and Ann Sochat, available from Tony Cano Enterprises, PO Box 220205, El Paso, Texas 79913. We've had excellent results at home and elsewhere with this recipe that is now more 'heart healthful' for us.

> \- The Two B's Dutch Oven Team
> Bill & Beverly Brummel
> San Antonio, TX

Steak 'N Taters 'N Veggies

12 inch Dutch oven - Serve 8 - 10 adults or 4 teenagers

3 lbs round steak, ½ inch thick
¼ cup regular, all-purpose flour
4 tsp salt
½ tsp pepper
¼ tsp garlic salt
¼ cup olive oil
1 lb baby carrots, whole or cut into halves
1½ lbs new red potatoes, cut into eighths
1 envelope onion soup mix
3 ½ cups water
chopped parsley for garnish

- Cut meat into servings pieces, trimming fat and bone. On wooden board, pound mixture of flour, salt, pepper, and garlic salt into meat.
- Set up Dutch oven to cook with 25 briquets on bottom.
- Pour oil into oven and brown meat well on both sides.
- Place carrots and potato chunks on top of meat. Sprinkle with onion soup mix and cover with hot water. Remove Dutch oven from briquets. Cover the oven and arrange 17 of the hot briquets on top of lid. Rearrange the remaining 8 bottom

Steak 'N Taters 'N Veggies continued . . . . .

Steak 'N Taters 'N Veggies continued . . . . .

    briquets and return oven on top of them. Bake for 1 ½ hours or until meat is fork-tender. You will need to fire up 12 new coals and replenish the used coals after the first hour of cooking by adding 4 fresh briquets on the bottom and 8 fresh briquets on the lid.
- Skim off any excess fat. If you so desire, thicken gravy with 2 Tbsp flour mixed with ¼ cup cold water and slowly stir into Dutch oven and bake for a few more minutes. Sprinkle parsley on top. Serve hot with buttered biscuits and enjoy!
- For indoor cooking, carry out steps 3 and 4 over your stove. Then bake in a covered casserole dish in conventional oven for 1 ½ to 2 hours at 350°F.

Historical Note

This is another recipe adapted from *Dutch Oven Cooking with Tony Cano*. Like all of our other Dutch oven recipes, we have slightly modified this one to be more 'Heart Healthful' for our needs. This is an excellent one pot recipe where all of the ingredients complement the others and makes for delicious eating for your family or company.

                         - The Two B's Dutch Oven Team
                              Bill & Beverly Brummel
                                  San Antonio, TX

Steak and Gravy

14 inch Dutch oven

2 lbs steak
flour
1 cup oil
1 can cream of mushroom soup
1 can water
salt & pepper, to taste
1 cup bell pepper, chopped
1 cup onion

Beef

a little garlic
a little Pace® Hot Picante Salsa
2 cups potatoes, diced
Cut meat into pieces. Fry until brown in oil. Remove meat. Add onion, bell peppers, and garlic, fry until brown. Add potatoes. Combine soup and water and pour over meat mixture. For a little added zip, add some Pace® Picante Salsa, to the soup mixture. Cook about 1 hour.

I cook in a 14 inch Dutch oven with about 12 coals on bottom and about 10 coal on top.

- Beverly Modgling
Medina, TX

Sweet & Sour Beef & Cabbage

12 inch Dutch oven - Serves 10

1½ lbs good ground beef
1½ cups onions, chopped
1½ tsp salt
1 tsp black pepper
1 - 12 oz jar Heinz® Chile Sauce
½ cup grape jelly
2/3 cup water
1 Tbsp low salt beef granules
8 cups or more cabbage, coarsely chopped

Mix salt, black pepper, chili sauce, water, grape jelly and beef granules. Warm to desolve grape jelly. Set aside. Place oven over 15 briquets. When hot, sauté onions & beef. Drain & remove from oven. Add about 2 inches of cabbage in bottom of oven. Place onions & beef mixture on top of that, then add enough cabbage to completely fill Dutch oven. Then pour grape jelly and chili sauce mixture over cabbage.

Sweet & Sour Beef & Cabbage continued. . . . .

Lone Star Dutch Oven Society Cookbook

Sweet & Sour Beef & Cabbage continued......

Place oven over 15 briquets & place 8 briquets on lid. Baste after 40 minutes. Cook another 20 minutes. It should be ready to serve.

> - Tom Payne
> Sulfur Springs, TX

Texas Hash

12 inch Dutch oven - Serves 8 - 10 adult folks

1½ lbs 80% lean ground beef
2 bell peppers (one green, one yellow), diced
2 large onions, diced
2 cans tomatoes, diced
1 cup white rice, uncooked
1 ½ tsp chili powder, or to taste
1 tsp salt
2 cups torn bread or bread crumbs

Sauté meat, peppers & onions until meat is browned & veggies are tender using 19 briquets coals under oven.
Add tomatoes with liquid, rice, and seasonings.
Add 2 cups of water.
Cook until rice is done & most of moisture is absorbed.
Add extra hot water during cooking, if necessary.
Top with buttered torn bread pieces or bread crumbs & bake using briquets only on top of lid until the bread is crispy.
Garnish as desired (we use cheese "stars") just before serving.
Serve hot and enjoy!

Historical Information

This is a recipe that we've used in our family for over 40 years as a casserole dish and now in Dutch ovens. We've found it to be an excellent 'one-pot' dish and by using very lean meat, a 'heart healthful' one.

> - The Two B's Dutch Oven Team
> Bill & Beverly Brummel
> San Antonio, TX

Texas Stuffed Steak

12 inch Dutch oven - Serves 8 - 10

3 lbs boneless round steak, ½ inch thick
2 Tbsp butter
2/3 cup celery, chopped
½ cup onion, chopped
2 1/3 cups (½ inch) bread cubes
½ tsp salt
1/3 tsp rubbed sage
½ tsp black pepper
1 ½ Tbsp water
all-purpose flour
3 ½ Tbsp vegetable oil
1 - 10¾ oz can cream of mushrooms soup, undiluted
2½ tsp Worcestershire sauce
1½ cloves garlic, minced
½ cup water

Trim fat from steak. Pound steak to 1/4 inch thickness, and cut into 4 equal pieces. Melt butter in 12 inch Dutch oven. Sauté celery and onion in butter until tender. Remove from heat. Stir in bread cubes, salt, sage, pepper and 1¼ Tbsp of water. Place 1/4th of mixture on each piece of steak, spreading to within 1/2 inch of edge. Roll up each piece jelly-roll fashion, secure with wooden toothpicks, and cut in half crosswise. Dredge each steak roll in flour and brown in hot oil. Combine soup, Worcestershire sauce, garlic, and 1/2 cup water. Stir well and pour over steak rolls. Cover and simmer 1 hour, stirring occasionally.

- Shem Ray, Jr. & Shem Ray, III
Sulphur Springs, TX

Famous "Wagon Wheel Roast"

12 inch Dutch oven
Will Fill Six Hongry Outlaws!

1 - 3 to 5 lbs chuck or other roast
1 - 14 oz bottle ketchup
1 - 12 oz bottle of beer
1 cup brown sugar, packed
1 tsp black pepper
1 tsp salt or to taste
1 onion, minced
1 tsp garlic, chopped
6 carrots
6 small peeled potatoes

ASSEMBLY INSTRUCTIONS:
- Start 25 or so charcoal briquets.
- Brown the meat in 2 Tbsp of fat.
- Mix all ingredients except vegetables and add to browned beef.
- Put lid on oven with 10 - 12 coals on bottom and 12 - 16 coals on top and roast for 2 hours (try not to burn it).
- After 2 hours or so, add the peeled carrots and potatoes and cook 30 minutes more.
- Present dish with roast centered on the lid and carrots and potatoes surrounding meat in a wagon wheel fashion.
- Serve with plenty of the sauce

ENJOY

Historical Note

This recipe was stolen from a famous Dutch oven cook named Jack Ware of Memphis, Tennessee at a cookoff in Greyhawk Frontier Village near Cabot, Arkansas. Ware told me that he stole the recipe from Colonel Tom Parker, Elvis Presley's manager and early mentor. Col. Parker was an avid camper and Dutch oven cook throughout the hills of Tennessee and Arkansas. Parker claimed he got the recipe from a Mississippi river boat captain back in the early 1900's.

- From the *OutLaw Gazette*
Hole in the Wall Press
Sulphur Springs, TX
Captain Joe Scott, editor

Beef

Twice Stuffed Dutch Oven Peppers

14 inch Dutch oven - Serves 12 - 15
Approximate cooking time 1 hr. 30 mins.

Preheat heat a 14 inch and a 12 inch Dutch oven approximately 400°F by **1 rings*** of coals on bottom and **2 ring*** of coals on lid.

5 bell peppers	5 fresh mushrooms
2 cups water	2 Tbsp chili powder
1 lb ground beef	1 Tbsp oregano
3 potatoes, diced	1 Tbsp garlic salt
1 medium onion, diced	2 beef bouillon cubes
2 - 30 oz cans tomatoes	1 small box Beef Rice-O-Roni®
	(2 Tbsp margarine)
	(2½ cups hot water)

- Clean and cut bell peppers in half
- Place peppers in pre-heated 14 inch Dutch oven with the skin side down.
- Add 2 cups of water and steam until tender
    (should take about 10 - 15 minutes).
- Remove peppers from the Dutch oven and set aside for later.

While the peppers steam prepare the following ingredients:
- In the 12 inch Dutch oven use **2 rings*** of coals under the pot.
- Brown 1 pound ground beef (drain off fat)
- Add the following to the same 12 inch Dutch oven and cook until tender, with **1 ring*** under the pot and **2 rings*** on lid.

3 potatoes	1 medium onion
2 Tbsp chili powder	5 fresh mushrooms, sliced
2 tsp garlic salt	1 Tbsp oregano
2 30 oz can tomatoes	2 beef bouillon cubes
(chopped w/juices)	

While that 14 inch Dutch oven is still warm prepare:
- Beef Rice-O-Roni® (according to the box instructions)
- Cook with **1 ring*** of coals under the pot and **1½ rings*** on lid.
- Combine cooked rice with items prepared in the 12 inch Dutch oven
- Spoon rice/meat/potato mixture into the bell pepper halves

Twice Stuffed Dutch Oven Peppers continued. . . . .

Twice Stuffed Dutch Oven Peppers continued. . . . .
- Replace the stuffed bell pepper halves into the bottom of the 14 inch Dutch oven.
- Continue to cook the 14 inch Dutch oven with stuffed peppers, Using a **1 ring*** of coals on the lid and **1/2 ring*** of coals on the bottom
- Cook for an additional 30 minutes

Historical Note
I made up this recipe on a camp-out trying to use up left-overs.

> \- The Cherokee Chefs
> Bonita & Felicia Sanders
> Seabrook, TX

*See 'Dinwiddie Method of Charcoal Briquet Use' on page 10.

Veal Cutlet Parmigiana
12 inch Dutch oven - Can serve 8 people, however, this is prepared for 5 people.

5 veal cutlets (3" x 5")	¼ cup green onion, chopped
1 cup flour	Marinara sauce (recipe follows)
2 eggs, beaten	5 slices Prosciutto or other thinly sliced ham
1 cup fine bread crumbs	
¼ cup olive oil	5 thin slices of Mozzarella cheese
¼ cup butter	
dash of salt	5 Tbsp Parmesan cheese
¼ tsp pepper	

Pound veal thin. Dip each in flour and then into egg wash and press bread crumbs in. Place in the olive oil and butter, sauté on each side for about 5 minutes. Add chopped green onions. Remove cutlet to oven lid and spoon equal amounts of sautéed onion on each. Prepare Marinara sauce. Once done, pour into pan. Lay cutlets on bottom of oven, spoon a little marinara on each and cover each with a slice of

Prosciutto and a slice of Mozzarella. Salt and pepper to taste. Spoon marinara on meat to cover. Bake at 375°F oven for about 1/2 hour, with 18 briquets on the top and 8 on the bottom. Sprinkle with Parmesan cheese.

Marinara Sauce

6 Tbsp olive oil	dash of salt
¼ cup butter	1 - 3 lb can tomatoes
3 large cloves garlic mashed	3 Tbsp dried oregano
16 fresh parsley sprigs	1 tin anchovy fillet, chopped
½ tsp black pepper	2 heaping Tbsp tomato paste

Slowly cook the garlic and parsley in olive oil and butter for about 5 minutes. Add pepper and salt. Drain tomatoes and chop the solids. Add tomatoes and oregano to sauce and cook slowly for 30 minutes. Remove from heat and add tomato paste and anchovies. Salt to taste.

- Thomas & Sue Williamson
Sulphur Springs, TX

Notes

Notes

Chicken & Poultry

Baked Turkey and Herb Stuffing

15 inch MACA Dutch oven - Serves 8 to 12

12 lbs turkey, giblets removed, rinsed and patted dry
2-3 Tbsp vegetable oil on paper towel, rub over entire turkey
salt & pepper to taste

STUFFING:
1 cup Pepperidge Farm® Corn Bread Stuffing (add more if stuffing appears too moist)
1 cup Pepperidge Farm® Classic chicken stuffing
1 cup celery, finely diced
½ cup onion, finely diced
½ stick butter or margarine

In 8 inch Dutch oven, sauté onion and celery in butter until onions are transparent.
Add the following ingredients to the 8 inch oven containing the onions and celery. Heat until bouillon granules are dissolved and water is hot. Then add liquid to a bowl containing the dry stuffing ingredients and toss well:
    1 cup water
    1 tsp chicken bouillon granules
    3 Tbsp seasoning from Classic Chicken Stuffing package

After stuffing the turkey, tuck legs into skin flap at the tail or tie the legs with string.

- Preheat the oven, for 15 minutes with **2 rings** of fresh charcoal on bottom and **2½ rings** on top. Then place the stuffed turkey inside on a cake rack to keep it up out of the juices that will accumulate. Allow the turkey to brown at high temperature for 30 - 45 minutes, then remove **1 ring** of charcoal from the bottom.
- At 1 hour remove the oven from the coals, dumping all the old charcoal. Place fresh charcoal **1½ rings** on top and **1 ring** on the bottom. (You may need more charcoal on the top if it is windy.)

Chicken & Poultry

- Continue cooking for 1½ to 2 hours more, basting the turkey as needed. Replace charcoal at 1 hour intervals, or more often as needed if it is windy.
- When the turkey is done, remove the lid, dump the charcoal and air cool it 15 minutes, then place the inverted lid on a lid stand. Place the turkey on the lid and garnish as desired. We prepare the lid with a bed of leaf lettuce first, then we garnish using a variety of fruits, such as grapes, strawberries, spiced peaches and spiced apple rings.

- Dos Dinwiddies
Duane & Sandy Dinwiddie
Houston, TX

*See 'The Dinwiddie Method of Charcoal Briquet Use' on page 10.

Cheesed Ham 'n Chicken with Confetti Rice

12 inch Dutch oven - Serves 9 adults or 3 teenagers

3 pieces - skinless, boneless chicken breast, cut into thirds across their width
9 slices - H.E.B's 95% Fat Free Mesquite Smoked Turkey Ham
1 cup white rice, uncooked
1/3 cup wild rice, uncooked
1 cup mixed red, green, and yellow bell peppers, diced
1 cup carrots, uncooked, peeled and sliced
5 cups chicken broth or chicken bouillon equivalent
9 pinches Cheddar cheese, shredded

- Wrap a slice of turkey ham around each chicken breast folding in a neat packet. Mix rice and vegetables in bottom of Dutch oven, pouring broth over all.
- Place meat packets on top of vegetables with seam side down (may have to use a toothpick to hold seam closed).

Cheesed Ham 'n Chicken with Confetti Rice continued. . . . .

Cheesed Ham 'n Chicken with Confetti Rice continued. . . . .

- Cook at 400°F with **15 briquets under and 14 on top** for about one hour or until liquid had been absorbed by vegetables and rice. After 30 minutes of cooking, **add 10 fresh briquets under and 5 on top**. May have to remove meat packets every so often and stir the other ingredients so they do not stick to oven's bottom. Add *hot* water if necessary during cooking.

- About 5 minutes prior to being done, lightly sprinkle shredded cheese over each meat packet and return lid to top of oven to slightly melt cheese. When done, remove any toothpicks, serve meat packets on top of veggies, and enjoy!

Historical Note

This recipe has been modified from an old casserole recipe of ours for use in Dutch ovens. Like all of our Dutch oven recipes, we've adapted this one to be more 'heart healthful' by using low sodium chicken broth or bouillon and low-fat products. The taste is most excellent! For use in your home's oven, cut this recipe in half and use a casserole dish with lid. This recipe is fit for your most important company or for impressing others!

> \- The Two B's Dutch Oven Team
> Bill & Beverly Brummel
> San Antonio, TX

Chicken 'n Dressin' 'n Veggies

14 inch Dutch oven - Serves 6 - 8

8 chicken breast halves, skinned and boned
6 to 8 yellow crooknecked squash
8 oz mushrooms, medium to large caps
¼ cup cooking oil
¾ cup Muenster cheese, grated
1½ cups chicken stock, divided use

1 - 6 oz can crab meat	1 cup bread crumbs
½ cup celery, diced	¼ cup butter, melted
2 cups cornbread, crumbled	4 eggs
3 - 4 slices light bread, dry	¼ cup onion, diced
1 tsp garlic powder	4 Tbsp red bell pepper, diced
2 to 4 jalapeno peppers (optional)	1 Tbsp dried rubbed sage

- Pound chicken breasts until thin. Sprinkle with fresh ground pepper and rub pepper in with palm of hand.
- Set up Dutch oven to cook with **25 briquets under the pot.** Melt butter in a cup in the oven. Remove cup. Pour ¼ cup oil into heat.
- In large bowl, mix cornbread, crumbled light bread, celery, red bell pepper, onion, sage, crab meat, garlic powder. Pour in melted butter, 2 eggs, and enough chicken stock to hold shape (approximately ¾ cup). Salt and pepper to taste. Place 2 Tbsp corn bread dressing in center of each chicken breast. Spread evenly on meat. Roll each breast up (like jelly roll) and secure end with toothpicks. Beat 2 eggs lightly in shallow bowl. Dip rolled chicken breasts in beaten egg, then in bread crumbs. Brown on both sides in hot oil. Pour ¼ - ½ cup chicken stock into pot.
- Remove oven from heat. **Put lid on oven and move 17 briquets from the bottom to the top of the lid. Rearrange the 8 remaining bottom briquets and place the oven over them.** Bake for 30 - 45 minutes.
- Scrub the yellow squash and slice in half lengthwise. Scoop seeds out of squash with spoon. Sprinkle with garlic salt and pepper. Place 1 - 2 Tbsp of cornbread dressing in squash.

Chicken 'n Dressin' 'n Veggies continued. . . . .

Chicken 'n Dressin' 'n Veggies continued.....
- Remove lid of oven and arrange squash around chicken breast rolls.
- Sprinkle the grated Muenster cheese over the chicken breast rolls and squash.
- Pour additional chicken stock around chicken and squash.
- Replace lid on oven and cook for 20 - 30 minutes.
- Wash and stem mushrooms. Pat dry and stuff mushroom caps with 2 - 3 tsp cornbread dressing.
- Remove oven lid. Arrange mushrooms on top of chicken rolls and squash. Replace lid and cook for additional 20 - 25 minutes or until all items are tender and the liquid is reduced and thick.
- Jalapeno peppers may be sliced and put either inside with the dressing or on top of chicken rolls.

                              - Oven Lovin' Team
                              Judy & Jamie Ragland
                              Duncanville, TX

Chicken 'n Rice

12 inch Dutch oven - 8 - 9 servings

8 - 9 skinless chicken thighs
2 Tbsp olive oil
1 cup rice
1 cup carrots, diced
¼ cup red & green bell pepper, diced
1/3 cup wild rice, uncooked
5 cups chicken broth and water, or chicken bouillon

- Preheat Dutch oven with 10 briquets on the bottom.
- Brown thighs in oil, remove from oven and set aside to drain on paper towels.
- Wipe out oven with paper towels.
- Put rest of ingredients in pot and add chicken on top.

- Cook at 400°F with 10 briquets under and 19 on top for about 1 hour until done. (May have to add hot water if necessary during cooking.)
- Stir the rice & veggies mixture every now and then to prevent burning.

Serve warm and enjoy!

Historical Note

This is an old family recipe we've used in casseroles for over 40 years that we've recently adapted for cooking in Dutch ovens. Like all of the Dutch oven recipes that we've adapted for our own use, this recipe is "heart healthful".

- The Two B's Dutch Oven Team
Bill & Beverly Brummel
San Antonio, TX

Chicken & Italian Sausage Cacciatora

12 inch Dutch oven - Serves 6 - 8

1 - 5 lb roasting hen, skinned and cut into serving pieces then lightly salted and peppered, to taste
1½ lbs mild, Italian sausage, cut into 3 inch lengths
1 large green, bell pepper, cut into large pieces
1 large red, bell pepper, cut into large pieces
1 large yellow onion, cut into large pieces
8 oz fresh mushrooms, rinsed and cut into thick slices
4 large cloves garlic, coarsely minced

SAUCE INGREDIENTS
1 - 29 oz can tomato sauce
1 - 14½ oz can Del Monte® original, stewed tomatoes, drained
1 - 6 oz can tomato paste
1 tsp Lawrey® Season Salt

Chicken & Italian Sausage Cacciatora continued. . . . .

Lone Star Dutch Oven Society Cookbook

Chicken & Italian Sausage Cacciatora continued......
1 tsp sweet basil
2 tsp Italian seasoning
1½ tsp fennel seed
3 tsp dried parsley

Fry sausage in Dutch oven over a ¾ spread of charcoal with a little oil until brown and fully cooked, approximately 20 -25 minutes. Then remove from oven and set aside. While sausage cooks mix together the sauce ingredients. Clean out oven, removing all stuck sausage residue and grease. Lightly re-oil oven. Place chicken in bottom of oven. Add half of each color of pepper, and all of the onions and garlic. Pour sauce over all. Cook over medium heat (**1 ring*** bottom, **1½ rings*** on top) at a brisk simmer for 45 minutes stirring occasionally. Add the rest of the peppers, sausage, and mushrooms. Mix them into the sauce well. Cook for another 25 minutes at a brisk simmer. (Add charcoal as necessary to maintain heat).
Garnish with fresh parsley, if desired.

- Dos Dinwiddies
Duane and Sandy Dinwiddie
Houston, TX

*See 'The Dinwiddie Method of Charcoal Briquet Use' on page 10.

Chicken Angelico

14 inch Dutch oven - Serves 8 - 10 regular folks,
4 - 5 Hongry ones

8 chicken breast halves, boned & skinned
1 cup Italian bread crumbs
½ tsp garlic salt
4 Tbsp margarine
¾ lb Muenster cheese, grated
8 oz fresh mushrooms, cleaned & sliced

2 eggs, beaten
½ tsp black pepper
1½ cups chicken broth

Mix bread crumbs with garlic salt and pepper. Set up Dutch oven to cook over 25 briquets. Melt margarine in oven. Dip chicken breast halves in beaten eggs and coat with crumb mixture. Brown in margarine until lightly browned on each side.

Spread half of the sliced mushrooms over the chicken breasts. Sprinkle the grated cheese on top of this. Add the remaining mushrooms. Pour chicken broth over all.

Remove Dutch oven from briquets. Cover the oven and arrange 17 of the briquets on the top of the lid. Rearrange the remaining 8 bottom briquets and place the Dutch oven over them. Bake for 40-45 minutes or until chicken is tender and the liquid is reduced and thick.

To expand recipe for a crowd or to create a one-dish meal, peel and quarter baking potatoes (approximately 4 - 5 for a 14 inch oven) and scraped and halved carrots (approximately 8 - 10) can be added after the chicken breasts have been browned. Baking time should remain the same but additional briquets may be needed.

Historical Note

Adapted from *Dutch Oven Cooking with Tony Cano* by Tony Cano & Ann Sochat. Published by Tony Cano Enterprises. P.O. Box 220205, El Paso, TX 79913.

- The Oven Lovin' Team
Judy & Jamie Ragland
Duncanville, TX

Chicken Chilaquiles Explorador

12 inch Dutch oven - Serves 8

¾ cup vegetable oil
15 corn tortillas cut into ½ inch lengths
3 cups shredded cooked chicken
3 cups shredded Monterey Jack cheese

EXPLORADORES GREEN SAUCE:
1½ cup onion, finely chopped
6 Poblano chilies, seeded and finely chopped
2 jalapeno chilies, seeded and finely chopped
1½ cloves garlic, finely chopped
3 Tbsp vegetable oil
¾ cup whipping cream
¼ tsp salt

- Place onion, chilies, garlic and oil in Dutch oven over medium heat, stirring occasionally until onion is translucent. Stir in whipping cream and salt, reserve.
- Place chicken and oil in Dutch oven over medium to high heat and cook until brown. Remove chicken, shred & reserve it.
- Place tortilla strips and oil in Dutch oven over high heat and cook until light golden brown, 30-60 seconds; drain and reserve.
- Grease bottom of Dutch oven, then heat by placing 14 coals on bottom and 8 coals on top.
- Layer half of the tortilla strips in bottom of oven; top with chicken, half of the Explorador Green Sauce and 1¼ cups of cheese. Gently press layers down. Repeat with remaining tortilla strips, sauce and cheese.
- Bake for 30 - 45 minutes until cheese is golden brown.

- Exploradores Dutch Oven Team
Bill & Cindy Williamson
Allen, TX

Chicken & Poultry

Cranberry/Orange Glazed Cornish Hens with Pecan Herb Stuffing

14 inch Dutch oven - Serves 3 - 6

3 Cornish hens, rinsed, giblets removed & discarded
pinch of salt & pepper
2 medium acorn squash, cut in half, seeds removed
6 half-ears corn on the cob
3 Tbsp butter or margarine
6 Tbsp brown sugar

Cranberry/Orange Glaze:
½ cup cranberry sauce, jellied
½ cup orange juice concentrate
½ cup light Karo® syrup

Pecan Herb Stuffing:
Combine in a medium bowl:
1 cup Pepperidge Farm Corn Bread Stuffing
1 cup Pepperidge Farm Distinctive Classic Chicken Stuffing with
 1 Tbsp seasoning from packet
½ cup celery, finely diced
¼ cup onion, finely diced
½ cup pecans, finely chopped

Heat the following together and when butter and bouillon are melted, add to stuffing ingredients:
1 cup water
½ stick butter or margarine
1 cube chicken bouillon

- Light enough charcoal for **1 ring*** and **1 full spread***, plus 10 briquets.
- Rinse hens in cold water and drain. Prepare stuffing.
- Sprinkle hens with salt and pepper, inside and out, then loosely fill the cavity with stuffing.

Cranberry/Orange Glazed Cornish Hens continued. . . . .

Lone Star Dutch Oven Society Cookbook

Cranberry/Orange Glazed Cornish Hens continued. . . . .
- Place stuffed hens in the oiled oven, evenly spaced apart, with the legs toward the outside of the oven.
- Place the oven over **1 ring*** of freshly lit charcoal and cover the top with a **full spread***. The high heat from the top will brown the hens.
- While hens are browning, prepare glaze by combining ingredients and beating with a wire whisk. (It will be slightly lumpy.) Also prepare three of the squash halves by placing 1 Tbsp butter and 2 Tbsp brown sugar into the hollow centers. Make sure the halves will sit level in the oven.
- When chickens are browned (30 minutes), add the 3 acorn squash halves between the chickens. Apply the glaze to the chickens with a pastry brush and re-glaze every 10 - 15 minutes. Remove enough coals from the lid so that **1½ rings*** remain along the outside rim. At 40 minutes, add enough charcoal to the 10 briquets left in the starter to make **1 ring*** of fresh coals.
- At 50 minutes into the cooking, add **½ ring*** fresh coals to both the top and bottom of the pot, add the corn, standing them on their ends between the hens and the squash around the outside.
- All should be perfectly cooked at 1 hour and 10 minutes. Garnish with and red spiced apples.

                       - Dos Dinwiddies
                       Duane & Sandy Dinwiddie
                       Houston, TX

*See 'The Dinwiddie Method of Charcoal Briquet Use' on page 10.

Chicken & Poultry

Dutch Oven Roasted Chicken

14 inch Dutch oven - Serves 8 - 10

2 medium size whole chickens
McCormick® Roasted Chicken Seasoning

Wash chickens inside and out. Remove any excess fat and trim any unnecessary skin. Pat chickens dry with a paper towel. Completely cover chickens inside and out with McCormick® roasted chicken seasoning (be liberal and generous with the seasoning). Fold the wings behind the neck to hold down any loose skin covering the chickens breast. Then tie the legs together with twine. When cooked these chickens tend to fall apart, so it is a great help if you bind them in this manner.

Place a trivet or rack in the bottom of the Dutch oven. Place the chickens on the rack, breast side up. Place a full bed of coals under the Dutch oven and a full bed of coals on the top. The chickens will cook very fast in the beginning. As cooking continues, the outside of the skin should be crispy and turn golden. Check after about 15 - 20 minutes to make sure that the breast is not turning too dark too quickly; if it is take some coals off the top. Total cooking time is 45 minutes to 1 hour.

When the chicken is done let it rest and cool down for about 20 minutes before you cut and serve it. To cut the chicken for servings: slice the thigh and leg off in one piece, and continue through the wing joint so that you end up with a half of breast with the wing attached, this will give you about 4 more servings. If the breast is a little dry cover it with the drippings from the bottom of the pan.

Historical Note

This is a recipe that I came up with one Sunday afternoon while experimenting in the back yard. It always comes out crispy on the outside but moist and tender on the inside. When properly cooked the chicken should just fall off the bones.

- The Hatfield Ranch Cocineros
Dan Hatfield & Cindy Rather
Median, TX

East Texas Chicken "Luzianna"

12 inch Dutch oven - Serves 6 hungry campers
32 briquets (18 to start)

3 - 5 strips smoked bacon, coarsely chopped
1 - 2 Tbsp olive oil
1 - 2 Tbsp butter
6 boneless chicken breasts (skin on)
1 cup flour, lightly seasoned with salt, black pepper, garlic powder & onion powder
1 cup onion, chopped
1 cup bell pepper (green, red, yellow, mixed), chopped
½ cup celery, finely chopped
1 Tbsp garlic, minced
2 - 6 oz cans lump crab meat with juice
2 - 6 oz jars artichokes hearts, quartered
1 - 6 oz can chicken stock (as needed)
½ cup heavy cream

To season to taste you will need:
salt, black pepper, dry basil, oregano, garlic powder, onion powder and Louisiana® Hot Sauce

Preheat Dutch oven with 12 - 18 briquets under the bottom.

Render bacon then remove meat and set aside. Add to the drippings 1 - 2 Tbsp each olive oil and butter. Season chicken breasts to taste with salt, black pepper, dry basil, and Lousiana® Hot Sauce. Dust breasts in seasoned flour (salt, black pepper, garlic powder, onion powder) shake off excess. Brown chicken breast (skin side down first). Remove breasts and drain excess oil from the Dutch oven.

Sauté onion, bell peppers, celery and garlic until onion is clear or translucent. Add chicken back into Dutch oven; top with crab, drained artichokes, rendered bacon. Season to taste with salt, pepper, oregano and add cream. Place lid on Dutch oven and add 10 - 12 briquets to the lid. Check briquets under the bottom, you need 8 - 10 to simmer. Simmer until done and sauce is thickened, approximately 30 - 40 minutes.

Chicken & Poultry

Add chicken stock as needed for liquid throughout cooking.
Garnish at serving with chopped parsley and/or crab claws.

Historical Note

This recipe was given to me by Matt & Brian Shuler of Wylie, Texas and is a great example of Texas/Louisiana style cooking.

- The Chuckle Wagon Cookers
Steve & Jeanice Bias
La Marque, TX

Explorador Jambalaya

12 inch Dutch oven - Serves 6-8

4 Tbsp margarine	1 tsp dry mustard
1¼ lbs smoked sausage	1 tsp ground red pepper
2½ lbs chicken, diced	½ tsp cumin
4 small whole bay leaves	½ tsp black pepper
1½ cups onions, chopped	½ tsp thyme
1½ cups green bell peppers, chopped	1 tsp white pepper
1½ tsp garlic, minced	1 tsp salt
2 cups white rice, uncooked	
4 cups water	

In oven melt margarine over a **¾ spread*** of briquets. Add the sausage & chicken and cook 5 minutes, stirring occasionally. Add remaining ingredients & brown, stirring occasionally. Add rice & chicken stock and cover. Remove enough charcoal under pot to leave **1 ring*** under pot. Top with **1 ring*** of briquets. Cook until rice is tender but crunchy.

- Exploradors Dutch Oven Team
Bill & Cindy Williamson
Allen, TX

*See 'The Dinwiddie Method of Charcoal Briquet Use' on page 10.

"Forever" Chicken
14 inch Dutch oven - Serves 8

1 Tbsp bacon drippings or 6 - 8 strips thick sliced bacon
8 pieces chicken (I prefer boneless skin on breast, but it can be any pieces and/or bone in.)
1 cup flour, seasoned with salt, pepper, garlic powder and onion powder
2 large onions, coarsely chopped (can include whole pearl onions or green onion bulbs with chopped onions)
1 - 2 Tbsp garlic, chopped
30 oz of your favorite **sweet** BBQ sauce (see below)
chicken stock - amount depends on how long you cook it
garnish with bell pepper strips and green onion tops.

If using bacon, render bacon and remove meat to side. Bring oven with drippings in it to browning temperature (at least 12 briquets under oven). Dust chicken with flour, shake off excess. Brown chicken (skin side down first). Remove chicken and keep warm on the side with bacon. Sauté onion, bell pepper, garlic in oil/juice in oven. Return chicken and bacon. Cover with BBQ sauce. {If using hotter/spicier sauce, add brown sugar, honey or corn syrup to sweeten.) Add chicken stock (or water) if sauce thickens too much. Use 12 briquets under and 16 briquets on top to start. Cook 1 hour (to 18 hours). maintaining medium low heat. Garnish at serving.

Bar-B-Que Sauce

64 oz catsup
1 cup dark molasses
½ cup white vinegar
½ cup prepared mustard
¾ cup brown sugar

2½ oz liquid smoke
1½ oz Worcestershire
1 Tbsp chopped garlic
½ Tbsp garlic powder
hot sauce, to taste

This is an easy, "no cooking required" sauce. It's our favorite. Of course, you can adjust the amounts to suit your taste.

Historical Note

When trailing cattle, one thing every cow hand got plenty of was beef. When they could get it, chicken was a welcome change. This is called "Forever" Chicken because it could be started with the coals from breakfast, cooked at low heat all day (often buried in the

Chicken & Poultry

ground) while the hands were working the range, and be perfect for supper. Even the night hawks coming to camp past midnight had a great hot meal. The chicken only gets more tender.

> - Shuler Land and Livestock Company
> Brian & Matt Shuler
> Wylie, TX

Garlic Turkey

14 inch deep Dutch oven - Serves 6 - 8

7 - 9 lb turkey	1 onion
1 green pepper	salt & pepper
8 cloves garlic	stuffing
¼ cup olive oil	

Quarter green pepper and onion and place in 14 inch deep Dutch oven pot with salted and oiled turkey. Insert 4 - 6 peeled and halved garlic cloves under skin of turkey leaving remaining cloves in turkey.

Bake turkey on trivet at 325°F (8 - 10 coals on bottom and 15 - 18 coals on top) for 15 - 20 minutes per pound or until done. Baste every 20 minutes while baking.

> - Don Cody & James Jones
> Medina, TX

Golden Baked Stuffed Chicken

12 inch deep Dutch oven - Serves 4 - 6
Approximate total cooking time - 2 hours

5 to 6 lb chicken, giblets removed, rinsed, patted dry with paper towel
2 Tbsp vegetable oil, on paper towel, rub over entire chicken
salt & pepper to taste

HERB STUFFING:
½ cup Pepperidge Farm Corn Bread Stuffing®
½ cup Pepperidge Farm Classic Chicken Stuffing®
½ cup celery, finely diced
½ cup onion, finely diced

Heat the following together and when butter and bouillon are melted, add to stuffing ingredients and toss well:
1 cup water
½ stick butter or margarine
1 tsp chicken bouillon granules
1½ Tbsp seasoning from Pepperidge Farm Classic Chicken Stuffing®
After stuffing the chicken, tie the legs together.

- Light enough charcoal for **2 rings*** on bottom and **2½ rings*** on top plus 10 briquets. You will **preheat the oven** getting it **very hot.** Then place the stuffed chicken inside on a cake rack to keep it up out of the juices that will accumulate.

- At 45 minutes add enough charcoal to starter for **1 ring*** on bottom and **1½ rings*** on top.

- At 1 hour remove the oven, dumping all the old charcoal. Place fresh charcoal on top and bottom. At this time cut the string tying the legs together so that they can open up slightly to brown and cook the inner thighs.

- Continue cooking for 1 hour. Chicken should be done and ready to remove. Garnish as desired.

Chicken & Poultry

We place the chicken on the lid that has been prepared with a bed of lettuce. We use a variety of fruits for garnish, such as grapes, spiced peaches, and spiced apple rings.

- Dos Dinwiddies
Duane & Sandy Dinwiddie
Houston, TX

*See 'The Dinwiddie Method of Charcoal Briquet Use' on page 10.

Granny Lemley's "Hens in the Herb Patch!"

12 inch Dutch oven - Serves 4 to 6

3 lbs chicken, cut up or 6 chicken parts
2 lbs mushrooms
4 Tbsp butter
4 Tbsp flour
2 cups beef broth
salt & pepper to taste
2 dried bay leaves or 3 fresh bay leaves
1 tsp ground sage or 6 leaves chopped fresh sage
1 tsp whole rosemary or two sprigs fresh rosemary
¼ tsp dried thyme or 1 tsp fresh thyme
2 Tbsp dried parsley or 3 Tbsp chopped fresh parsley

Melt butter in oven over medium heat, approximately 8 coals on the bottom. Slice mushrooms and sauté in butter. Brown chicken pieces and remove to plate. Mix flour into butter and cook a few minutes. Add broth gradually, stirring continually. Simmer, stirring occasionally, until sauce thickens. Add all herbs except parsley. Salt and pepper to taste. Return chicken to oven. Spoon sauce over chicken. Sprinkle parsley over all.

Granny Lemley's "Hens in the Herb Patch!" continued. . . . .

Granny Lemley's "Hens in the Herb Patch!" continued. . . . .

Cover and bake for one to two hours or until chicken is tender. Keep heat at approximately 350°F by keeping 8 - 10 coals on the bottom and 17 coals on the lid. Give pot a quarter turn every 15 to 20 minutes. At the same time turn the lid a quarter turn in the opposite direction as the oven.

Historical Note

This recipe has been handed down in the our family from one generation to the next. We usually serve it with baked potatoes or rice.

- The Prairie Kitchen
Cheryel Lemley
Covington, TX

Holiday Chicken

12 inch or larger Dutch oven - Yield 12 servings
Use 20 briquets on bottom of oven, only
Cooking time approximately 1½ hours

4 whole chicken breasts - boned and cut into ½ inch squares
2 eggs
1 cup milk
3 cups flour
3 tsp salt
2 cups lard
2 green peppers, cut into 1 x ½ inch strips
6 salad tomatoes, cut into wedges
30 oz pineapple bits

Mix eggs and milk in a bowl. Mix flour and salt in another bowl. Dredge chicken in flour mixture, then in milk mixture, then repeat in flour. Place chicken on waxed paper.
Place lard in Dutch oven, then add the chicken. Cook until done.

Chicken & Poultry

Sauce:
6 Tbsp oil
2 cups vinegar
2 cups brown sugar
4 Tbsp garlic salt

4 Tbsp soy sauce
8 Tbsp corn starch
5 cups water

In a 12 inch Dutch oven or larger, combine oil, brown sugar, vinegar, and garlic salt: at moderate heat, until sugar is dissolved. Combine corn starch with 1 cup of water, add to sugar mixture, stirring constantly until corn starch begins to thicken. Add remaining 4 cups of water and continue stirring. Add soy sauce and cook until brown and the consistency of cream sauce, approximately 10 minutes.

Combine cooked chicken and green peppers with sauce, cover and cook 5 minutes. Add pineapples and tomatoes, cover and cook another 5 minutes.

Historical Note

This recipe has been used by Mr. Murphy at several cook-off's and has earned him several hundred dollars and a trip to the national cookoff. It can be made smaller or larger depending on how much of the ingredients you use.

- Frank Murphy
Houston, TX

King Ranch Chicken Casserole
14 inch Dutch oven - Serves 6 hungry Cowboys

6 chicken breasts	12 corn tortillas
2 medium onions	1 cup Cheddar cheese, grated
1 tsp black pepper	1 cup Monterey Jack cheese,
½ tsp garlic salt	1 green bell pepper
1 large can cream of chicken soup	
1½ cups tomatoes, chopped	olive oil
3 Serrano peppers, finely chopped	

Fill Dutch oven half full of water, add chicken, 1 chopped onion, 1 tsp black pepper, ½ tsp garlic salt. Place Dutch oven over hot coals (about 20 coals) and bring to a boil, allow to cook (covered) until chicken separates from bone (cooks in about 30 minutes).

When chicken is done, take chicken from water discarding bones and skin. Chop chicken into coarse chunks and set aside. Take 2 cups of chicken broth from Dutch oven and set aside in a medium size bowl (discard remaining broth).

Sauté 1 chopped onion and ½ chopped bell pepper, in small amount of olive oil in Dutch oven. Combine chopped chicken, cream of chicken soup, chopped tomatoes, fine chopped Serrano peppers, with sautéed onion/pepper. Remove mixture from oven, place in a medium bowl.

Dip each corn tortilla in chicken broth. Use tortillas to line bottom of Dutch oven. Pour chicken mixture on top of tortillas in Dutch oven. Cover mixture with cheese. Place lid on oven. Cook with 20 coals on top and 5 coals on the bottom. Cook for 30 - 45 minutes until cheese browns. Garnish with bell pepper slices.

Historical Note
The original King Ranch Casserole was developed by a woman from Robstown, Texas about 20 miles north of the King Ranch, many years ago. Since that time many variations have developed. The King Ranch has never at any time dealt with the raising of chickens. The King Ranch is a National Historic landmark. It is recognized as the birthplace of the American ranching industry. Founded by

Chicken & Poultry

Captain Richard King in 1853, King Ranch developed the Santa Gertrudis and King Ranch Santa Cruz breeds of cattle and produced the first registered American Quarter Horse. Today, King Ranch sprawls across 825,000 acres of South Texas land, an area larger than the state of Rhode Island. As the home of 60,000 cattle and 300 Quarter horses, King Ranch is one of the largest ranches in the world today.

- James & Toni Clark
Corpus Christi, TX

"Little Chicken with Big Eyes"

Serves 6 hungry campers
14 inch Dutch oven
32 briquets (22 top/12 bottom = 375°F)
Total cooking time 1½ hours

3 Cornish game hens (1½ lbs each)
2 boxes Pepperidge Farm® Wild Rice & Mushroom Dressing
2 - 4 oz cans mushroom pieces & stems
3 medium white onions (1015 are best)
6 Tbsp Worcestershire Sauce
9 Tbsp butter or margarine

- <u>Prepare onions</u>: peel outer skin, cut funnel shapes out of bottom of onions and fill each with 1 Tbsp butter and 1 Tbsp Worcestershire sauce. Set aside
- Preheat Dutch oven with 12 briquets under the bottom. Place Game Hens (without giblet packets) in oven and place a onion between each hen. Place lid on Dutch oven and add 22 briquets to the top. Cook for 45 minutes.
- <u>Prepare Dressing</u>: In a large bowl place the vegetable seasoning packet from the Pepperidge Farm® Wild Rice & Mushroom Dressing with 2½ cups boiling water let stand for 15 min. Add 6 Tbsp butter or margarine. Mix well. Add dressing mix and drained mushrooms. Mix well, set aside.

"Little Chicken with Big Eyes" continued. . . . .

Lone Star Dutch Oven Society Cookbook

"Little Chicken with Big Eyes" continued. . . . .
- After hens and onions have cooked for 45 mins. Place the dressing around them and cook until the onions become very soft (30 - 45 min.). Add briquets as needed to keep the Dutch at 375°F (adding briquets about every 20 - 30 minutes).

- The Chuckle Wagon Cookers
Steve & Jeanice Bias
La Marque, TX

"Mary Goodell's Honey Salsa Chicken"
12 inch Dutch oven - Serves 4 - 6

3 - 4 lbs chicken, cut up	¼ cup salsa
1 Tbsp butter or margarine	½ cup honey
1 onion, chopped	dash of Tabasco® sauce
2 tsp chili powder	1 Tbsp soy sauce
2 Tbsp prepared mustard	½ tsp seasoned salt

Begin with **2 rings*** of charcoal briquets under Dutch oven. Melt butter in Dutch oven and then add the onion, chili powder, mustard, seasoned salt, salsa, honey, Tabasco® sauce and soy sauce. Simmer for 5 minutes to blend flavors and soften onion. Remove from heat, add chicken, dipping meat into the sauce until all pieces are well coated.

Place oven over **1½ rings*** of briquets, with **2 rings*** of briquets on the lid. Check pot every 15 - 20 minutes, to check for even cooking and to baste the pieces. Cooking time is about 1 hour.

Historical Note

This recipe is a favorite of a good friend of mine from Idaho. Mary Goodell was her mother. It has been adapted from a conventional oven recipe. If you want to cook this in your oven at home bake at 350°F for about 1 hour.

- Nancy Alemany
Sugar Land, TX

*See 'The Dinwiddie Method of Charcoal Briquet Use' on page 10.

Chicken & Poultry

Old Fashioned Chicken and Dumplings

"This recipe is simple for the beginner and can be adjusted for any size oven."

14 inch oven - serves 7 - 8
Serving size: 2 Thighs & Dumplings

14 - 16 skinned chicken thighs
Water
4 - 5 carrots sliced
salt & pepper

cooking oil
1 - 2 medium onions, sliced
2 - 3 stalks celery, chopped

Salt and pepper chicken, cover the bottom of a 14 inch Dutch oven with the cooking oil. Heat oil with 14 -16 coals under the oven, brown the chicken and onion in the oven. When the chicken and onions are browned, cover the chicken with water, bring to a light to medium boil by adding 6 - 8 coals to the bottom and one ring on the lid. Cook for 1 hour to 1½ hours or until chicken is tender. Then add the carrots, celery and any other spice desired. While this is cooking start your dumplings.

DUMPLINGS

1 1/8 tsp yeast
¼ cup warm water
1 Tbsp sugar
1 Tbsp baking powder
¼ tsp baking soda

2 Tbsp melted shortening
½ tsp salt
1 cup buttermilk
3 cups flour

Dissolve yeast in warm water, mix all ingredients together. Knead lightly. Make into 2 inch dough balls and flatten to ½ inch thick. Drop dumplings in the pot. Keep at a low boil or simmer after the dumplings are added. Cook for 20 to 30 minutes or until the dumplings are done. Add heat to top and bottom as needed.

- Todd & Sissy Sandidge
Bandera, TX

"Pecos Jack's World Famous Roast Yard Bird with Orange and Honey Sauce and a few select Garden Vegetables"

14 inch Dutch oven - Feeds one mountain man or six adults

Two young tender yard birds without feathers
Two medium onions
Six small ears of sweet corn
Two yellow & Two green summer squash
½ cup honey
One medium. can frozen orange juice
One small can mandarin oranges
Fiesta®Brand - garlic, chicken fajita seasoning, & Cajun seasoning
Potatoes, carrots, pimento peppers and black pepper

In a 14 inch deep Dutch oven place two washed real good young tender yard birds without any feathers at all on them. Heat at 350°F (12 briquets under pot, 16 briquets on top), for 20 minutes just to get them warmed up good and started cooking up and then add range sauce of 1 medium can frozen orange juice with ½ cup honey. Dust yard birds real good with Fiesta® garlic & fajita seasoning. Continue to cook for twenty more minutes. After forty minutes add two medium onions, two yellow & two green squash. Add six small ears of corn and dust lightly with Fiesta® Cajun seasoning. During first forty minutes baste with orange sauce from bottom of the pot. Cook yard birds and vegetables together for another 30 minutes, total cooking time 1 hour 10 minutes or until yard birds are brown, tender and juicy.

Historical Note

Pecos Jack was a mountain man who came to Texas about 1875 from the Rocky Mountains and spent the rest of his life living on the wild Pecos River in Val Verde County, Texas. He died alone on the Pecos river and his remains have not been found to this day. While he was living no farmer's yard birds in Val Verde County were safe.

- Jack Richardson,
Sugar Land, TX

Polly Ryon's Prairie Chicken Pie

12 inch Dutch oven - 8 - 10 Servings

THE PIE:
2½ lbs boneless, skinless chicken, cut in 1 inch cubes.

2 Tbsp olive oil	3 cups chicken broth
2 medium onions	3 ribs celery, diced
2 lbs mushrooms in 1 inch pieces	1 ½ tsp ground cumin
1 lb carrots, cut into ¼ inch dice	½ tsp cayenne pepper
6 jalapeno peppers, seeded and minced	2 Tbsp flour

THE CRUST:

3 cups water	1 cup milk
2½ tsp salt	1½ tsp baking powder
1½ cups yellow cornmeal	¼ tsp ground pepper
3 Tbsp butter	½ cup grated Cheddar cheese
3 eggs, separated	
2 large scallions, thinly sliced	

With 12 briquets underneath the oven, heat 1 Tbsp of olive oil. Add the chicken and sear until browned, about 5 minutes. Transfer the chicken to a bowl. Place 2 tsp of oil in the oven and add the onions, carrots, celery and jalapenos. Sauté for 8 minutes. Add broth. Stir in the mushrooms and cook for 5 minutes. Stir the chicken into the vegetable mixture. Stir in the remaining broth, cumin, cayenne, 1½ tsp of salt and pepper. Stir ¼ cup of the stew liquid into the flour, then stir the mixture back into the stew.

To make the spoon-bread crust, bring the water to a boil in a 10 inch Dutch oven. Add the salt. Whisking constantly, pour the cornmeal in a slow, steady stream. Whisk for 20 seconds and remove from the heat. Place in large bowl, mix in the butter and let cool. In another bowl, whisk together the egg yolks, milk, baking powder and pepper. Gradually stir the egg mixture into the cornmeal mixture. Stir in the cheese and scallions. Whip the egg whites until stiff but not dry. Fold into the cornmeal mixture. Spread the spoon bread over the chicken mixture.

Polly Ryon's Prairie Chicken Pie continued. . . . .

Polly Ryon's Prairie Chicken Pie continued.....

Cook at 400°F in Dutch oven, placing 14 - 16 briquets on the lid and 12 - 14 underneath the oven for 45 minutes.

Historical Note

This is a recipe from the foreman of Polly Ryon's cattle and land company. Prairie chickens are prevalent, easy to shoot, and tasty.

- Los Cocineros de Arroyo Seco
Carl S. Hacker & Claudia A Kozinetz
Houston, TX

Powder River Pat'ridge

12 inch Dutch Oven - Feeds 6 hongry outlaws

4 boneless, skinless partridge (or chicken) breast halves, flattened & cut into cutlets
1 cup pecans, ground with 2 Tbsp flour
1 beaten egg
2 Tbsp butter
2 tsp fresh thyme (1 tsp dried)
½ pint heavy cream
¼ cup hazelnut liqueur
1 small can mandarin oranges, drained
fresh parsley and orange slices for garnish

ASSEMBLY INSTRUCTIONS:
- Start 25 or so charcoal briquets.
- Melt 2 Tbsp butter in oven.
- Pound bird breast filet to exactly 10/32" thickness and cut into 2" x 3": tournedos and season with salt and pepper to taste.
- Dip cutlets into beaten egg and roll in pecan flour mixture to coat.
- Sauté cutlets in butter until light brown, remove from oven.

Chicken & Poultry

- Add cream, hazelnut liqueur, thyme and mandarin oranges to oven. Boil slightly to thicken. Return bird to oven. Place a few coals on the lid and cook 5 minutes until done.
- Garnish with fresh parsley, orange slices and serve with plenty of sauce.

Historical Note

This recipe was given to me by Paula Hanson, wife of Brock Hanson. They have a ranch on the Red Fork of the Powder River near Kaycee, Johnson County, Wyoming. Paula is the descendant of a pioneer family who homesteaded this land back in the mid 1800's. Her great-grandfather settled the land and was there when the battle of Dull Knife occurred. Dull Knife was the Chief of a group of Indians camped on the Powder River and were attacked by a company of 7th Cavalry soldiers. After a fierce battle with many casualties, Dull Knife lead his people to safety out of the canyon by a secret draw that lead over the top of the mountain. Other members of the Hole in the Wall Gang and I have trout fished this land many times. The land abounds with Partridge, Chukar and Quail as well as trout and large game. Paula, who is not known for her cooking, said the recipe was one given to her by her grandmother.

- From The OutLaw Gazette
Hole in the Wall Press - Sulphur Springs, TX
Captain Joe Scott, editor

Sherried Emu

14 inch Dutch oven - 14 - 1 cup servings
Preparation Time: 1 hour 30 minutes

3 lbs Emu
2 ½ cups water
1 cup sherry wine, medium dry
8 Tbsp soy sauce
6 large carrots, sliced
12 ounces sugar snap peas

Sherried Emu continued. . . .

Lone Star Dutch Oven Society Cookbook

Sherried Emu continued....
3 large green bell peppers
3 medium onions
6 Tbsp vegetable oil
3 Tbsp cornstarch
4 - 6 oz pkgs. long grain and wild rice, prepared by package directions.

Slice Emu into ½ inch strips. Combine water, sherry, and soy sauce. Pour over Emu strips in dish; marinate one hour. Slice carrots, peppers, and onions. Stir-fry carrots for 2 - 3 minutes in half of the vegetable oil then add the remainder of vegetables to a 14 inch Dutch oven. Over medium-high heat, about 20 coals on the bottom, cook vegetables until they are tender-crisp remove from oven and set aside. Drain Emu strips; reserve marinade. Brown Emu strips in remaining vegetable oil, do not over cook Emu, it takes no more than 5 minutes to brown. Combine cornstarch with reserved marinade in bowl. Add to Emu strips and cook stirring, until thickened. Add vegetables to Emu strips. Cook five minutes longer with 20 coals on pre-heated lid. Combine with cooked long grain and wild rice.

- Paul & Sissy Garrison
Median, TX

South of the Border Chicken

12 inch Dutch oven - 12 servings

2 cans Campbell's® Fiesta Tomato Soup
2 cans chicken broth
1 cup water
2 cups long-grain rice, uncooked
12 skinned and boned, chicken breast halves
2 cups coarsely crushed tortilla chips
1 cup grated Cheddar cheese

Chicken & Poultry

Combine soup, broth, water and rice in a greased 12 inch Dutch oven. Bake over medium heat; (10 coals under and 12 coals over) for 20 minutes. Arrange chicken over rice mixture and bake an additional 25 minutes. Sprinkle chips and cheese over chicken and bake an additional 5 minutes or until cheese melts. If you like extra spice, add a couple of chopped jalapeno peppers to the soup, rice and broth mixture.

- Shem & Norma Ray
Sulphur Springs, TX

Southwest Chuck-Wagon Chicken

12 inch "deep" Dutch oven
Serves 6 - 8
Approximate total cooking time = 2 hours

8 slices thick-sliced, bacon, cut into 1 inch pieces
3 Tbsp vegetable oil
1 - 5 lb roasting chicken, cut into serving pieces, skin left on
1 cup seasoned flour (½ tsp salt, 1 tsp each pepper, paprika)
2 large onions, coarsely chopped
6 cloves garlic, crushed
2 - 14 oz cans stewed tomatoes, chopped up juice included
2 - 4 oz jars chopped pimentos, drained
6 oz frozen peas
2 red, bell peppers, coarsely chopped, stems and seeds removed
3¾ cups water
3 tsp paprika
3 tsp salt
1 tsp poultry seasoning
1 tsp cumin, ground
1 tsp chili powder
1 tsp cayenne pepper
2 cups long-grain rice, uncooked
1 bunch fresh parsley, garnish
lemon slices, garnish behind the parsley
Southwest Chuck-Wagon Chicken continued. . . . .

Southwest Chuck-Wagon Chicken continued......

- Light enough charcoal to set up **one full spread*** plus **1 ring and 10 briquets***. When the coals are ready, place the Dutch oven over the a **full spread***, add the oil and bacon, and put the lid on with **1 ring*** on it. Fry bacon with frequent stirring until crispy, about 10 minutes, then remove.
- While bacon is cooking, coat **chicken** in the **seasoned flour**.
- After removing the bacon, add the **chicken pieces** to the hot oil, skin side down, and brown on both sides (about ten minutes per side), with the hot lid on the pot.
- When you turn the chicken the first time (about 20 minutes into the cooking), add enough charcoal to the 10 burning briquets in your starter to make **four rings***.
- While the chicken browns, add together in a bowl, the **water, paprika, salt, poultry seasoning, cumin, and chili powder**, mixing well to blend the spices.
- When the chicken is lightly browned on both sides, remove it to a plate. (The chicken will not be completely cooked at this time.)
- Remove all but about 1 Tablespoon of the oil and bacon drippings from the Dutch oven and discard, leaving any flour stuck to the oven.
- Pour into the Dutch oven; the water with the spices, adding the **onions, garlic, canned tomatoes, pimentos, peas, peppers, and rice**, and gently stir with a wooden spoon to mix all ingredients well.
- At this point, the charcoal you added to your starter should be fully lit. <u>Replace</u> the bottom coals with **1 ring*** of fresh lit charcoal, and <u>replace</u> the lid with **1½ rings***. The other lit coals are backup if it gets windy.
  Cook about 25 minutes, or until about half the water is absorbed by the rice.
  Stir well and add the **browned chicken**, arranging it about half buried into the other ingredients.
- Cover and cook 45 minutes to an hour more, with further stirring. Near the end, add charcoal as necessary to keep up a good simmer and steam. Dish is done when rice is tender and water is absorbed.
- Garnish by shaking some paprika onto the chicken pieces, and adding **sprigs of parsley** and half slices of **lemon**.

Chicken & Poultry

- Dos Dinwiddies
Duane & Sandy Dinwiddie
Houston, TX

*See 'The Dinwiddie Method of Charcoal Briquet Use' on page 10.

Sunday Best Roast Chicken
14 inch Dutch oven - Yields: 8 servings
Approximate cooking time: 3 - 4 hours

Preheat a 14 inch Dutch oven to approximately, 400°F by **1 rings*** of charcoal briquets on bottom and a **2½ rings*** on the lid.

2 - 3 lbs chicken
2 Tbsp garlic powder
2 Tbsp salt
2 Tbsp lemon pepper
a handful of green snap beans

8 small red potatoes
2 cups carrots
4 large ears of corn
1 large red bell pepper

- Clean chickens and coat all sides and inside with garlic powder, salt and lemon pepper.
- Place chickens in pre-heated Dutch oven with the breast up.
- Cook for 30 minutes per pound of chicken, with **2½ rings*** of coals on lid and **1 ring*** on the bottom.

While chicken cooks, prepare remaining ingredients
- Wash the vegetables. Peel and cut carrots into 2 inch strips.
- Cut corn into 1 inch thick wheels.
- Core the bell pepper and cut into 1 inch rings.
- Clean the snap beans and leave them whole.

One hour before serving time - remove the excess juice around chicken. Arrange vegetables in Dutch oven with the chicken. Continue cooking for the last hour.

Sunday Best Roast Chicken continued. . . . .

Lone Star Dutch Oven Society Cookbook

Sunday Best Roast Chicken continued. . . . .
- The Cherokee Chefs
Bonita & Felicia Sanders
Seabrook, TX

*See 'The Dinwiddie Method of Charcoal Briquet Use' on page 10.

Turkey Pot Pie
14 inch "deep" Dutch oven
Feeds 10 - 14 people

PASTRY
6 cups all-purpose flour
2 tsp salt
2½ cups shortening
2 eggs, well beaten
10 Tbsp cold water
2 Tbsp apple cider vinegar

Combine flour and salt; cut in shortening until mixture resembles coarse meal. Combine eggs, water and vinegar; mix well and stir into flour mixture. Turn pastry out onto a lightly floured surface, knead until you have a good texture. Set aside 1/3 of the pastry for the top of the pot pie. Roll out the rest of the pastry on a floured surface to 1/4 inch thickness, approximately 3 to 4 inches larger than the lid of the Dutch oven. Place the pastry in a well greased 14 inch Dutch oven, pressing the pastry evenly up the sides of the oven.

(Hint: it may be easier to cut the pastry in quarters and place it in the oven so that the pieces overlap then press them back together.)

FILLING
2 lbs cooked turkey breast, diced into 1/2 inch cubes
1 - 15 oz can of Veg-All®, drained
1 - 29 oz can of Veg-All® (Home style Large Vegetables), drained
1 - 8 oz can Le Seur® Sweet Peas, drained
1 - 10¾ oz can Campbells® Cream of Mushroom Soup
1 - 10¾ oz can Campbells® Cream of Potato Soup
1 - 10¾ oz can Campbells® Cream of Chicken Soup

Chicken & Poultry

1 - 10½ oz can Campbells® Chicken Broth
½ tsp pepper
1 tsp McCormick Season All®

Combine all of the above in a large bowl and pour into the pastry lined Dutch oven. On a floured board roll out reserved pastry to approximately the size of the Dutch oven lid. Place on top of the filling mixture, then seal the top and bottom crust together by pressing edges together and rolling them down the side of the oven.

Cook at approximately 375°F until golden brown (about 1 hour). Start with 16 to 18 coals on the bottom and 14 to 16 coals on the top. Place more heat on the top and less on the bottom about half way through the cooking process.

- The Hatfield Ranch Cocineros
Dan Hatfield & Cindy Rather
Median, TX

Wrapt Chicken

12 inch Dutch oven - Serves 10 - 12

6 chicken breasts, boned and skinned
12 pieces sliced cooked ham
12 pieces sliced Swiss cheese
1 can cream of chicken soup
½ cup milk
12 toothpicks

With a piece of chicken between 2 pieces of waxed paper or Saran Wrap®, pound meat to 1/4 inch average thickness, cut pieces in half. Do the same with the remainder of the chicken.
Ham and cheese slices should be about the same size as the chicken. Lay a slice of ham on the chicken, on top of the ham lay a slice of

Wrapt Chicken continued. . . . .

Wrapt Chicken continued. . . . .

cheese. Roll all together, jelly-roll fashion, and pin with a toothpick to keep from unrolling. Lay pieces on bottom of oiled oven. In bowl, mix soup with just enough milk to make a pourable mixture. Cover all the chicken rolls with the soup mixture.

Bake at 375°F for 60 minutes. Place 8 - 10 charcoal briquets under and 16 over. Remove heat from bottom of oven after 10 - 15 minutes to prevent burning. Garnish with parsley to serve.

Historical Note

This is somewhat uptown for typical cowboy fare but they sure lick their chops when convinced this is pretty darn good eatin'. No one knows who invented Cordon Bleu but it has been around for a good bit o' time.

- Larry & Bungy Hartshorn
Bandera, TX

Notes

Fish & Wild Game

Huntress Venison Stew

12 inch Dutch oven - Serves 6

1 lb deer steak, cut into 1 inch cubes
1 cup red table wine, preferably a Texas wine
1 - 6" sprig of fresh rosemary or 1 tsp dried
2 bay leaves, fresh or dried
1/4 tsp pepper
1 tsp salt
3 strips thick, smoked bacon cut into 1 inch pieces
1 - 16 oz can beef consommé
2 cups whole baby carrots, peeled
1 lb whole baby new red potatoes
1 lb fresh mushrooms, pick the smallest ones
1/2 lb whole pearl onions, peeled
1 Tbsp cornstarch
3 Tbsp cold water
1 - 16 oz can baby corn, drained

Combine first seven items. Marinate overnight.
Light 50 or more charcoal briquets. When coated with a layer of white ash, place 14 briquets under oven. Fry bacon in Dutch oven till just crisp. Drain meat and brown in oven. Add marinade with herbs and consommé. Lower heat to slow simmer by removing 4 briquets. Place lid on oven. Put 12 briquets on lid. Adjust briquets to maintain slow cooking for approximately 2 hours. Add water as needed if stew is cooking down too fast. Refrain from removing lid often, as this reduces heat and extends cooking time. The last hour add carrots and potatoes. The last half hour add onions and mushrooms. The last 15 minutes, combine cornstarch and water. Stir into oven to thicken stew. Add corn. Serve when corn is heated through. This is good with hot crusty bread and a good Texas red wine.

Historical Note

Some women have always loved to hunt and cook what they've bagged. This is my version of the traditional hunter's stew updated for '90's ladies.

- The Prairie Kitchen
Cheryel Lemley,
Midlothian, TX

Pioneer Shepherd's Pie

2 - 12 inch Dutch ovens - Serves 10 - 12 people

20 large potatoes
1 - #10 can, whole kernel corn
6 - 7 lbs beef or wild game, finely chopped or coarsely ground
1 large sweet onion, chopped fine
1 large green pepper, chopped fine
Several mushrooms, chopped or sliced (optional - This would depend upon whether or not wild edible mushrooms could be found in the logging vicinity.)
1 - 2 cloves garlic
5 tsp salt
1 tsp pepper
1 1/2 cups milk
1/2 lb butter or margarine (2 sticks)
1 tsp paprika
1 tsp dried parsley
5 - 6 quarts water

Peel potatoes and cut into quarters. Add 6 quarts of water. Add 1 - 2 tsp salt and boil until soft and tender (about 40 min., using 35 - 40 charcoal briquets). Empty water and place potatoes in a bowl or deep pan. Put potatoes through a ricer or mash. Add 3 - 4 Tbsp of butter and 1 tsp of salt. Add milk and beat until smooth and creamy. Set aside.

Using 18 - 20 briquets, heat Dutch oven in which potatoes were cooked. Grease with 2 tsps of butter or margarine. Add meat of your choice and brown. (Spoon off any excess grease.) Add onions - lightly chopped, green pepper - chopped small, sliced mushrooms; finely chopped garlic; 3 tsps of the salt; and 1 tsp of pepper.

When meat and vegetables are done, take oven off heat and smooth mixture out across bottom. Gently add corn as a layer over the meat mixture. Dot corn with approximately 4 briquets of butter or margarine.
Pioneer Shepherd's Pie continued. . . . .

Pioneer Shepherd's Pie continued . . . . .

Now carefully cover corn with the mashed potatoes. You now have a layer of meat, a layer of corn and a layer of mashed potatoes. Sprinkle the potatoes lightly with pepper and parsley.

Put oven back over 8 briquets, and on lid put 8 - 10 briquets. Leave for about an hour. Check meat every 10 - 15 minutes to be sure it is not burning on the bottom.

Historical Note

This comes from Uncle David's pad of recipes, and is an early American dish that has been a favorite among the early settlers from Maine to Texas to California. The basic food substances are meat, corn and potatoes. The meat may be anything from beef, pork, lamb, buffalo, bear, chicken, dove, deer, quail, or any combination of these meats.

                        - William & Marilyn D'Lizzarraga
                            Sulphur Springs, TX

Rabbit 'n Rice

12 inch Dutch oven - 8 Servings

4 cups brown or yellow rice
8 cups branch water (upstream from cows)
2 rabbits (skinned) or 8 chicken thighs
2 cans cream of mushroom soup
1 large onion

With a **full spread*** of briquets under oven sauté onion in lard or margarine. Salt and pepper meat to taste, add to onions and brown thoroughly. When meat is browned remove onions and meat mixture from Dutch oven. Set aside. Bring 8 cups of water to a boil. Add rice to water, bring water to a boil again. Add meat & soup to rice and water. With **1 ring*** of briquets on the bottom and **1½ rings*** on top of oven continue to cook until water has been absorbed and meat is cooked.
*See 'The Dinwiddie Method of Charcoal Briquet Use' on page 10.

Seafood Jambalaya

14 inch Dutch oven - Serves 15 - 18

1 to 2 lbs smoked sausage or cooked chicken
¼ cup olive oil
1 medium onion, cut into 1/8 inch slices
1 stalk celery, diced
1 carrot, julienned
2 cups mushrooms
4 medium tomatoes, diced
1½ cups uncooked rice
3 cups chicken broth
2 tsp paprika
½ tsp pepper
2 Tbsp salt
¼ tsp cayenne pepper
1/8 tsp saffron (or cumin)
2 cups shrimp
1 lb sea scallops
½ lb slipper lobster tails ("slipper" refers to the size)
1 - 10 oz pkg. green peas
1 - 15 oz can artichoke hearts
1 - 4 oz can pimentos, drains

In 14 inch Dutch oven, brown chicken in olive oil, using 18 - 22 briquets under; add onions, celery, carrots and mushrooms and cook for 5 minutes. Add rice, broth and next five (5) seasonings, simmer covered for 20 minutes. Add shrimp, lobster, scallops, peas and tomatoes and /or sausages; cover and simmer 15 minutes.
 Hint:
The pre-cooked little sausages work great in this recipe. Other seafood items may be substituted for ones listed. Adjust seasoning to suit your preference.

- The Oven Lovin' Team
Judy & Jamie Ragland
Duncanville, TX

Snapper Crack
12 inch Dutch oven - Serves 6

Fresh Gulf Snapper
oil (for cooking)
2 Tbsp butter
sesame seed
2 Tbsp mustard
1 cup white wine
wild rice
corn on the cob in 1 inch pieces

1 red pepper, sliced
1 jar artichoke hearts
1 medium onion, sliced
10 mushrooms, sliced
3 garlic cloves, crushed

Seasonings: garlic powder, onion powder, jalapeno salt, black pepper

Prepare rice - set aside
Bread Snapper in sesame seeds & a combination of the seasonings garlic powder, onion powder, jalapeno pepper, salt and black pepper to taste. Heat oil, then add sesame seed crusted snapper and vegetables - sweet red pepper, artichoke hearts, onions, mushrooms and corn on the cob over a **full spread*** of coals, until red pepper is tender crisp and the snapper coating is browned. Remove Snapper and vegetables. Add butter to Dutch oven with wine, mustard and crushed garlic cloves. Stir until thickened. Put rice, Snapper & vegetables back in Dutch oven, heat with **1 ring*** of coals on the bottom and **1½ rings*** on the top for 5 minutes and serve.

- Ann Marie & Shem Ray III
Pasadena, TX

*See 'The Dinwiddie Method of Charcoal Briquet Use' on page 10.

(Note: Fresh gulf snapper refers to any of the tasty fish in the snapper family, which can be caught off the Texas Gulf Coast.)

Fish & Wild Game

Toad Holler Frog Legs

14 inch Dutch oven - 10 - 12 servings

4 lbs frog legs (about 48 pairs)
2 to 3 sticks of butter
8 cups mushrooms
3/4 to 1 cup flour
6 to 8 cups chicken broth

salt & pepper, to taste
4 oz sherry, to taste
milk (to soak legs in)
extra flour to coat frog legs

Make sure the frogs are dead. If necessary, whack them on the head with a heavy stick. Skin and clean them. Soak the frog legs in milk for 1 hour.

Bring to a gentle sizzle 1 to 2 sticks of butter or margarine. Add and sauté until light brown on both sides: 8 cups of cleaned mushrooms, sliced or whole. Remove the mushrooms to a hot platter and add 1 more stick of butter or margarine to the drippings. (Make sure you have enough butter in the bottom of the pan to be able to cook the frog legs in. Do not add butter if it is not necessary.)
Salt & pepper the frog's legs and coat them with flour then sizzle them gently in the butter until they are browned on all sides. Put them on the hot platter with the mushrooms and then stir into the pan drippings 3/4 to 1 cup of flour. Stir in 6 to 8 cups of chicken broth and simmer and stir until smooth. Add 4 oz sherry (more or less to suit your taste). Add the frog legs and mushrooms back to the Dutch oven and stir them together. Serve while hot. This is a great dish served over hot wild rice.

Historical Note

One time when my father and I were in south Texas hunting, I caught a bunch of hoppers in an old stock pond. I cleaned them and took them back to camp for mom to cook that night. After several legs had hopped out of the pot when mom was cooking them, she turned around and told us, "If you want these damn frogs cooked then come cook them yourselves!" That is how I became the frog leg cook in our family.

- Hatfield Ranch Cocineros,
Dan Hatfield & Cindy Rather
Medina, TX

Venison Gumbo

14 inch Dutch oven - 8 - 2 cup servings

2 lbs venison, ground
2 Tbsp oil
2 - 15 oz can Hunts® tomato sauce
7 cups fresh tomatoes, chopped
6 cups fresh okra, sliced
2 medium bell peppers, chopped
1 large onion, chopped
2 large jalapeno peppers (or to taste)
salt & pepper
2 - 3 cups water

Preheat the 14 inch Dutch oven over 15 to 20 charcoal briquets. Add oil and meat when oven starts to get hot. Salt & pepper meat to taste and stir meat constantly so that the meat does not burn. When the meat is almost done add tomato sauce, tomatoes, okra, bell pepper, onion, jalapeno peppers and enough water to cover all the ingredients. Salt & pepper to taste. Cover with lid and stir occasionally. Place 5 to 6 briquets on the lid. Bring to a boil for 25 to 30 minutes or until the okra is done. Remove half of the coals to simmer for 15 - 20 minutes. Be sure and not let the water get too low or you could burn the bottom.

- Todd & Sissie Sandidge
Bandera, TX

Pork

Best of the Garden Pork Chops
14 inch Dutch oven

Serves 8 - 10 depending on how many pork chops you use
1 - 1½ hours cooking time - depends on thickness of pork chops 10 coals on the bottom & 14 coals on top

8 - 10 pork chops
2 Tbsp oil
1 cup rice, uncooked
1 large onion, sliced
2 - 3 bell peppers, sliced
2 - 3 tomatoes, sliced
¼ tsp marjoram
¼ tsp thyme
salt & pepper to taste
2 - 10 oz can beef broth

Preheat Dutch oven with 10 briquets under the Dutch oven; when heated for about 5 minutes add the oil and brown chops on both sides; arrange in oven. Sprinkle rice into spaces between chops. Top each chop with slices of onion, tomato and green pepper. Sprinkle with seasonings. Pour broth over top. Cover the Dutch oven and put 14 briquets on the lid. Bake for 1 hour or until chops and rice are tender.

Historical Note
When our summer garden starts producing we start cooking this dish. We hope that your family will enjoy it like we do.

- The Ewings
Allen, TX

Billy Bob's Wild West Ribs

12 inch Dutch oven - Serves 6 - 8

5 lbs country style ribs
½ cup ketchup
2 Tbsp Tabasco® sauce
1¾ cups chili sauce
2 medium onions, chopped fine
¾ cup vinegar
1/3 cup molasses
3 Tbsp Worcestershire sauce
1 tsp salt

In Dutch oven mix ketchup, chili sauce, onion, vinegar, salt, molasses and Worcestershire sauce. Add ribs and mix with sauce.

Put 12 briquets on bottom of oven and 24 on top.

Cook stirring occasionally until meat is very tender, about 1 to 2 hours. During cooking, add new coals on top and bottom as need to keep the heat up.

With baster, siphon fat from oven juices and discard.

- Bill Williamson
Allen, TX

Dutch Oven BBQ Pork Steaks

12 inch Dutch oven - Serves 3 - 4

Preheat 12 inch Dutch oven to approximately 400°F by using 10 - 12 coals on bottom and 14 - 16 coals on lid. (For a 14 inch Dutch oven double the recipe but only use 1/2 more coals.)

Cook in Dutch oven for 30 minutes:
3 lbs pork steaks (or chicken or beef steaks)

Combine:
1 - 14 oz bottle catsup
¼ cup beer
¼ cup vinegar
3 Tbsp brown sugar
1 Tbsp prepared mustard
3 Tbsp Worcestershire sauce
2 Tbsp chili powder
2 Tbsp smoked salt (or liquid smoke)
dash garlic salt
salt & pepper to taste

Pour grease from cooked meat.

Spoon BBQ sauce over the meat. Reduce the coals by ¼ and return meat to cook for an additional 1½ hours or until tender.

Historical Note
I like to use a 14 inch Dutch oven for my meat, stacking a 12 inch with a cake and a 10 inch with a vegetable on top. What a feast!

- The Cherokee Chef
Bonita Sanders
Seabrook, TX

Hill Country Spiced Peach Jam Steaks

14 inch Dutch oven - Serves 6 - 8

6 to 8 - ½ inch thick smoked pork shoulder ham steaks
½ cup brown sugar, firmly packed
1 lb 13 oz can Delmonte® Whole Spiced Peaches
4 oz Gulden's® Spicy Brown Mustard

Mix brown sugar and spicy brown mustard into a smooth paste. Wash and pat dry ham steaks then thoroughly spread mixture over both sides of ham steaks. Place small cake cooling rack into bottom of a 14 inch Dutch oven and layer ham steaks on top of rack. Place spiced peaches around ham steaks and pour remaining spiced peach liquid just up to the bottom of the cooking rack.

Bake at medium hot temperature (350°F) with approximately 10 - 12 coals on bottom and 15 - 17 coals on top for 15 - 20 minutes per pound of ham steak.

Historical Note
This is the perfect Easter Sunday after church lunch for friends or family to enjoy as the first outside meal of the year.

- Alan & Joyce Switzer
Fort Worth, TX

Night Riders' Supper

A One Course Meal

12 inch Dutch oven - Serves 8 - 10

6 cups potatoes, sliced ¼ inch thick, with skins
1 Tbsp cooking oil
1 medium yellow onion, diced
1 garlic clove, diced
1 green bell pepper, sliced
½ green or red chili pepper, diced
1 jalapeno pepper, diced
1 - 10 oz can RO-TEL® diced tomatoes & green chilies, with liquid
¼ cup pimento, chopped
1 cup celery, chopped
1 can (1 cup) cooked corn, drained
1 lb Cheddar cheese, shredded
½ tsp salt
4 cups cooked ham, small sliced pieces
3 cups Polish sausage, thin slices
2 cans cream of chicken soup, undiluted
3 eggs, lightly beaten
2 cups spinach, fresh, finely chopped
1 cup sour cream
½ cup corn flakes, crushed
6 parsley sprigs

New or red potatoes are best; wash, slice with skins, set aside. Sauté onions, garlic, bell pepper, chili pepper and jalapeno pepper in cooking oil. Add RO-TEL® mix, pimento, celery, corn, cheese, salt, ham and sausage slices. Add potato slices and mix well. Bake 1 hour in a moderate oven, about 350°F, using 15 charcoal briquets on top and 9 briquets underneath. Maintain this heat level during cooking period. If excess liquid appears, remove with a baster.

Top with crushed corn flakes and shredded cheese before serving. Garnish with parsley sprigs.

Historical Note

On the trail, cowpunchers had to work split shifts at night. The first from dusk to midnight, the other from midnight 'till dawn, as night riders. It was cold, hard and sometimes, wet work so the "cookie" kept a big pot of rib stickin' grub warmin' on the campfire. The ones' head'n out would grab a plateful first before head'n out. The one's comin' in, would scarf some down and hit the hay full as ticks. This midnight supper filled them and warmed their bellies for those cold nights.

- Larry & Bungy Hartshorn
Bandera, TX

Pecan-Apple Stuffed Pork in the Beans

12 inch Dutch oven - Serves 4 hungry campers

32 charcoal briquets
4 - 1½ inch thick pork chops
2 Granny Smith apples, peeled, cored and finely chopped
1 red delicious apple
½ cup pecans, finely chopped
2 Tbsp butter, melted
¼ tsp black pepper
1/8 tsp ground cloves
¼ tsp ground cinnamon
2 Tbsp brown sugar
1 - 2.6 oz can mushrooms
8 toothpicks

½ tsp salt
½ cup raisins
2 - 16 oz cans cut green beans, drained
1 - 10½ oz can cream of mushroom soup
1 - 2.8 oz can Durkee® French Fried Onions
¾ cup milk
1/8 tsp black pepper

Pork Chops and Stuffing:
Make a slit to form a pocket in the fat side of each pork chop. In a bowl, combine Granny Smith apples, raisins, pecans, brown sugar, cloves, cinnamon, pepper, and salt.

Add melted butter and mix well. Let stand for a few minutes for the flavors to blend.

Preheat Dutch oven with 18 charcoal briquets under the bottom.
Pecan-Apple Stuffed Pork in the Beans continued. . . . .

Pecan-Apple Stuffed Pork in the Beans continued. . . . .
Stuff each pork shop with a generous portion of stuffing. Skewer shut with toothpicks.

Heat butter in Dutch oven. Brown chops slowly for about 5 to 7 minutes on each side.

<u>Beans</u>
In a medium bowl, combine green beans, milk, soup, pepper and ½ the can of French Fried onions, set aside.

<u>In the Dutch oven</u>
Remove Dutch oven from heat. Remove and set aside pork chops. Drain the juices out of the oven. Cut a large hole in the top of the Red Delicious apple and fill with excess stuffing. Place apple in center of the oven. Return pork chops to the Dutch oven. Stand them on end with the slit pocket on top, making an "X" shape. Between each of the pork chops place equal amounts of the green bean mixture.

Place lid on Dutch oven and add the 18 used charcoal briquets to the lid, place 8 new briquets under the bottom. Bake for 20 minutes. (350°F) Add briquets as needed. Add to top of the beans the remaining onions. <u>Remove toothpicks from the pork chops!</u>

Bake for 10 minutes or until onions and chops are golden brown.

Makes 4 large servings.

      - The Chuckle Wagon Cookers
       Steve & Jeanice Bias
        La Marque, TX

Pork

Pineapple-Stuffed Spareribs

14 inch Dutch oven - Feeds 6 - 8 adults or maybe 2 teenagers

1 rack pork spareribs (about 3 lbs) cut to fit inside oven vertically
¼ cup chopped celery
2 Tbsp chopped onion
2 Tbsp butter/margarine or olive oil
1 Granny Smith apple, chopped
1 - 13 ½ oz can pineapple tidbits, drained (reserve syrup)
½ tsp ground cloves
2 cups packaged seasoned stuffing of your choice

- Start charcoal: you'll need 20 on top and 20 under to start.
- Tie spareribs in a circle using cotton twine.
- Spray a light coating of olive oil inside oven.
- Place charcoal briquets in a checker-board pattern both under pot and on the lid.
- Do not add water but place ribs in center of the oven with bone tips up, close lid and cook at 325°F for 2 hours, adding 16 new briquets on top and 5 new briquets on the bottom, as needed.
- In the meantime, cook and stir celery and onion in butter/margarine (we use olive oil) until tender.
- Mix celery/onions with pineapple, cloves, apple, stuffing, and enough reserved pineapple syrup to moisten.
- Spoon dressing mix loosely into circle of ribs. Place balance of dressing around the outside bottom of ribs.
- Continue cooking recipe for another 30 minutes or until meat is done.
- Slice between ribs, serving ribs with dressing and enjoy!

Historical Note

We call this recipe our "Poor-man's Pork Crown Roast". This recipe can be done inside your kitchen oven by using an indoor Dutch oven, or on a rack in a shallow roasting pan, using the same temperature and directions. Not only is this recipe very delicious, It's also very impressive to guests!

- The Two B's Dutch Oven Team
Bill & Beverly Brummel
San Antonio, TX

Pork Chops and Scalloped Potatoes

14 inch Dutch oven - Serves 6 - 8

Coals needed: Top - 22
Bottom - 10

Note: A very quick, easy, and tasty recipe. Careful with the black pepper, it is easy to overdo. You will need an extra Dutch oven, skillet or spider, with 12 extra lighted coals, to brown the chops and prepare the sauce.

2 lbs potatoes (about 8 - 10 medium), peeled if desired (we leave the skins on, they taste better and it's one less thing to do), sliced about 1/8 inch thick
2 medium onions, thinly sliced and separated into rings
6 stalks of celery, thinly sliced
3 tsp salt, divided
1 tsp ground black pepper, divided
½ cup all-purpose flour
6 - ¾ inch thick boneless pork chops
4 Tbsp vegetable oil
2 Tbsp all-purpose flour
1½ cups milk

- Light the coals to bake the recipe, plus 12 extra coals for step 3.
- Layer potato, onion and celery in Dutch oven until used up. Sprinkle with 2 tsp salt and ½ tsp pepper, set aside.
- Heat 2 Tbsp oil in extra Dutch oven, skillet or spider, you want the oil to be hot enough to just start smoking.
- Combine ½ cup flour, remaining 1 tsp salt, and remaining ½ tsp pepper; dredge the chops in flour mixture, brown in the hot oil. Add remaining 2 Tbsp of oil after 3 chops have been browned. Remove the chops as they brown, set them aside.
- Add 2 Tbsp flour to the drippings in the pan, continue cooking and stirring until smooth. Gradually add milk; cook, stirring constantly, until mixture is slightly thickened. Add more milk if too thick to pour easily.
- Pour mixture over vegetables; top with chops.
- Arrange 10 lighted coals for bottom heat, place oven over the coals; arrange 22 lighted coals on lid.

Pork

- Bake for an hour, or until the chops and potatoes are tender.

                              - Mike & Ed Galucki
                                      Cabot, AR

Pork Chops Old Home Style

14 inch Dutch oven - Serves 16 - 20

16 pork chops - loin cut preferred, 3/4 inch thick
salt & pepper
3 Tbsp cooking oil
8 Tbsp margarine
6 cups stuffing mix with seasonings
3/4 cup water
8 medium sized potatoes, quartered, peeled or unpeeled
12 - 16 carrots, scraped & halved
2 - 10 ¼ oz cans mushroom or cream of chicken soup
1½ cups water

- Preheat Dutch oven using 12 coals under and 16 coals on lid. After 7 - 10 minutes remove lid and place on a lid stand.
- Place cooking oil in oven. Salt & pepper chops to taste. Place chops in oven with cooking oil and brown well on each side.
- Melt margarine in bowl placed on Dutch oven lid.
- In large bowl mix stuffing mix, melted margarine, and ¼ cup water. Add more water as needed to make mixture moist enough to hold together.
- Shape stuffing mixture into small balls (golf ball size) and place on top of browned pork chops in Dutch oven.
- Place prepared potatoes and carrots around chops in oven. Pour cans of soup over top of food, add 1½ cups water and bake.

Cooking time will be approximately 50 - 60 minutes at 350°F. Check after first 20 minutes and gently lift and stir and add

Pork Chops Old Home Style continued . . . .

Pork Chops Old Home Style continued . . .
water as needed. Adjust number of coals to maintain moderate heat and keep food just above a simmer. Dish is done when vegetables are tender and gravy is thick and smooth.

This recipe can be served with corn bread or sourdough rolls, a favorite beverage and Sourdough Mountain Cobbler. Yummmmm!!!

Historical Note
Adapted from a recipe in the expanded 2nd edition of *Cooking the Dutch oven Way* by Woody Woodruff. Published by ICS Books Inc., 1370 E. 86th Place, Merrillville, IN 46410.

- The cooking team of
Jamie Ragland, Duncanville, TX
& Robin Bohls, Bastrop, TX

Pork Crown Roast

Deep 17 inch or larger Dutch oven
Feeds 14 - 18 people

1 - 12 to 14 lb pork rib crown roast
2 Tbsp snipped fresh thyme
2 Tbsp snipped fresh basil
2 Tbsp snipped fresh sage
1 Tbsp hot pepper sauce
½ tsp salt
½ tsp cracked black pepper
2/3 cup cane syrup or
　　½ cup dark corn syrup plus 2 Tbsp light molasses
1 - recipe of Sweet Pepper Stuffing (recipe follows)

- Preheat Dutch oven to 350°F. In a small mixing bowl combine thyme, basil, sage, hot pepper sauce, salt, and pepper; rub half of the mixture into the inside of the ribs. Set remaining herb mixture aside for stuffing. Place the pork roast on a trivet or

Pork

rack in a 17 inch or larger deep Dutch oven. Lightly spoon some of the stuffing mixture into the center of the roast.

- Insert a meat thermometer into roast so it is not touching bone or fat. Cover stuffing and rib tips loosely with foil. Roast in a 350°F oven for 2 hours or until meat thermometer registers 150°F. Remove foil; brush roast with some of the cane syrup or corn syrup and molasses. Roast about 15 minutes more or until thermometer registers 160°F and the meat is slightly pink in the center, brushing with remaining cane syrup. Let the roast stand for 15 minutes before carving.

- If desired cover the lid with Kale or lettuce and transfer the roast to the lid for serving. To serve cut down through the meat between ribs. Each rib and accompanying chop will make one main dish serving. Spoon out some of the stuffing with each serving.

Sweet Pepper Stuffing

12 inch or larger Dutch oven
Feeds 12 - 16 people

2 cups onion, chopped
2 cups celery, chopped
1 cup red sweet pepper, chopped
1 cup yellow sweet pepper, chopped
4 cloves garlic, minced
6 Tbsp margarine or butter
2 medium red or green apples, chopped
1 cup fully cooked Andouille sausage or smoked sausage, chopped
10 - 12 cups dried bread cubes
1 to 2 cans of chicken broth or water

- In a the 12 inch oven cook onion, celery, red pepper, yellow pepper and garlic in hot margarine or butter, covered over medium heat for 3 minutes. Add apple. Cook, covered for 6 to 8 minutes more or until ingredients are tender
- Stir in remaining herb mixture (see Pork Crown Roast recipe) sausage, green onions, and parsley. Remove from heat. Add bread cubes, toss gently to mix. Add chicken broth or water

Sweet Pepper Stuffing continued.......

Sweet Pepper Stuffing continued......

- to moisten. Do not make it wet and gooey; just sufficiently moist.
- Bake in the greased 12 inch Dutch oven at about 350°F for 30 - 45 minutes. The top will be slightly browned when ready. Place about 6 - 8 coals on the bottom and about 12 on the top to start with. For my bread cubes I like to use a combination of equal amounts of stale corn bread, old stale biscuits and toasted white or French bread.

Historical Note

These two recipes the Pork Crown Roast and the Sweet Pepper Stuffing are from Lafitte's Landing, Donaldsville, Louisiana. The notorious pirate John Lafitte once stashed his cache of riches and his two children at this Arcadian (Cajun) cottage hidden deep in the swampy bayous of Louisiana. His son, wanting none of his father's seafaring ways, grew up to marry the cottage builder's grand-daughter. The cottage is now a restaurant, and the great Cajun cooking is still enticing folks to stop by.

> \- Hatfield Ranch Cocineros
> Dan Hatfield & Cindy Rather
> Medina, TX

Stuffed Pork Tenderloin

12 inch Dutch oven - 4 - 6 servings

1 medium apple, chopped
6 - 8 prunes, chopped
2 slices dry bread, toasted and torn
1 tsp rosemary
1/2 tsp sage
2 - 3 tsp coarsely ground black pepper
3 Tbsp melted lard (butter may be substituted for 1990's style cooking)
2 slices bacon, cut into ½ inch pieces

Pork

3 large onions, peeled and sliced in rings
1 pork tenderloin

Stuffing mixture
Combine the apple, prunes, rosemary, sage, and ½ tsp of the coarse black pepper in a medium bowl. With 12 briquets on the lid and 18 underneath the oven, melt the lard (butter). Pour the melted lard (butter) over the stuffing ingredients and mix thoroughly. Place one slice of bread in the oven, cover and toast for 8 - 10 minutes. Place the second slice of bread in the oven, cover and toast for 8 - 10 minutes. Tear the slices of bread into ¼" pieces and combine in the bowl with the other ingredients.

Pork Tenderloin
Prepare the tenderloin by coating it with approximately 2 tsp of coarse black pepper. Slice the tenderloin lengthwise and place the stuffing between the slices then tie in place with cotton string.
Lightly fry
the bacon in the same Dutch oven used above. Cover the bottom of the oven with the sliced onions and place the stuffed tenderloin on top of the onions.

Cook (350°F) in the Dutch oven, placing 12 - 14 briquets on the lid and 10 - 12 briquets underneath the oven for 30 minutes. For an additional hour, cook with 12 - 14 briquets on the lid and 8 underneath the oven

Historical Note
This recipe was acquired by Mr. Samuel May Williams on a trip to Sao Paulo, Brazil. His cabin mate, Jan Dryselius, emissary from Sweden, prepared this delightful fruit stuffing three days out of Philadelphia when a hog was killed by a falling block, which had broken loose from the rigging.

- Los Cocineros de Arroyo Seco Cooking Team
Carl S. Hacker & Claudia A. Kozinet
Houston, TX

Tangy Bar-BQ Baby Back Ribs

12 inch Dutch oven - Serves 8 to 10

6 to 8 racks baby back pork ribs, cut into individual ribs
2 - 1.5 oz envelopes, Lantana® Bar B Que seasoning

Sandy's Bar BQ Sauce
1 - 20 oz bottle Heinz® Ketchup
1 - 12 oz bottle Heinz® Chili Sauce
1 cup brown sugar, firmly packed
½ cup honey
1 tsp balsamic vinegar
1 tsp Figaro® Mesquite Smoke Marinade
1 tsp Wright's® Liquid Hickory Smoke
2 tsp Lawreys® Seasoned Salt
2 tsp Lawreys® Seasoned Pepper
1 tsp Worcestershire sauce
½ cup Heinz® 57 Sauce

- Lightly rub Lantana® Bar B Que Seasoning on individual ribs and place in 12 inch Dutch oven on their sides, packed tightly. Continue until you have as many ribs as you desire. This recipe calls for 2 layers of ribs stacked on top of each other. (The dry seasonings give the ribs a little extra zing, helps the liquid sauce stay in place and alleviates the need to brown the ribs.)
- Cook with **1 ring*** of charcoal on the bottom and **1 1/2 rings*** on top (350°F), for about 1 hour.
- Then remove the top layer of ribs to a plate. Scoot the remaining ribs to one side and, while tilting the oven, absorb the rendered grease with a pair of tongs and paper towels, or use a turkey baster.
- Reposition bottom row of ribs, add about ½ cup of water to the pot, and brush on BBQ sauce. Return the removed ribs to the oven and brush on BBQ sauce. Cover with lid and continue cooking for 1 hour, adding water and basting with BBQ sauce as needed. The water steams the ribs without removing the sauce and prevents anything from burning. Never let the pot go dry. Ribs will be tender and ready to eat after 2 hours, but you can leave them in the oven for an additional 30 minutes, if this meets your needs, just keep them basted as needed.

Pork

Historical Note
This is an original recipe of ours. Hope you enjoy them as much as we do!!!

- Dos Dinwiddies
Duane & Sandy Dinwiddie
Houston, TX

*See 'The Dinwiddie Method of Charcoal Briquet Use' on page 10.

Notes

Notes

Side Dishes

Asiago & Sage Scalloped Potatoes

12 inch Dutch oven - Serves 8 - 10

2 Tbsp butter
2 medium onions, thinly sliced
1½ tsp garlic, chopped
2 bay leaves
¼ tsp nutmeg
1 Tbsp salt
¾ tsp pepper
1¼ cups heavy cream
½ cup milk
1 cup Asiago cheese - grated
1 cup bread crumbs - plain, dry
2 Tbsp olive oil
½ tsp sage, fresh (use less if dried)
¼ tsp salt
¼ tsp pepper
2½ to 3 lbs potatoes, peeled & sliced 1/8 inch thick
2 Tbsp sage - fresh (use less if dry)

Sauté onions in the butter over high heat for about 8 minutes.

Add to the sautéed onions; garlic, bay leaves, nutmeg, 1 Tbsp salt and ¾ tsp pepper. Cook 30 seconds. Then add cream and milk and bring to a boil. Remove from heat, cover and let stand for 5 minutes.

In a medium bowl, toss cheese, bread crumbs, olive oil, ½ tsp sage and ¼ tsp salt and ¼ tsp pepper. Set aside.

Remove bay leaves from onion/milk mixture and stir in 2 Tbsp sage. Combine the sliced potatoes and onion/milk mixture in a large bowl. Toss gently. Spread half of the potatoes in a greased 12 inch Dutch oven. Sprinkle with 2/3 cup of cheese/bread crumb mixture on top. Repeat with potatoes - press firmly to pack down. Cover this layer of potatoes and onions with remaining cheese/bread crumb mixture.

Bake for 45 minutes to 1 hour at about 400°F or until potatoes are tender and golden. If they brown too quickly, remove some coals from top of Dutch oven or loosely cover with foil.

Side Dishes

Historical Note

This is a recipe that Cindy came across at a friend's dinner party one night. She thought it was an excellent recipe, so we quickly set about converting it into a Dutch oven dish. It turned out to be a great Dutch oven dish and is not as difficult as it might seem by the ingredients.

- The Hatfield Ranch Cocineros
Cindy Rather & Dan Hatfield
Comfort, TX

Carrots Myway

12 inch Dutch oven - Serves 6 hungry campers

32 mesquite briquets (18 to start)
8 medium carrots
2 Granny Smith apples
2 Red Delicious apples
2 Tbsp butter
2 Tbsp butter, melted
1 small jar maraschino cherries
½ cup orange juice
½ cup brown sugar
1/8 tsp ground ginger
¼ tsp ground cinnamon
1 small bag of marshmallows

Wash carrots and apples. Peel carrots and cut into ¼ inch slices. Preheat Dutch oven with 18 briquets under the bottom. In the Dutch oven melt butter, add carrots, place lid on Dutch oven, and cook carrots for 20 minutes. Stir every 6 minutes

In a small bowl mix well: brown sugar, ground cinnamon, ground ginger, set aside. Core and slice apples into ¼" rings, set aside. When carrots have cooked for 20 minutes, add apple rings and drizzle orange juice over all. Sprinkle brown sugar mix over all. Set up Dutch oven with 17 briquets on top and 8 under the bottom (350°F) bake for 20 minutes. Remove Dutch oven from bottom briquets. Garnish carrot/apple mixture with marshmallows and maraschino cherries. Bake with briquets on top of Dutch oven for 10 minutes more. Serve 6 hungry campers, right from the Dutch oven

Carrots Myway continued . . . . . .

Carrots Myway continued......

Historical Note

I love to cook in the Dutch ovens and experiment with different recipes. The best time to do this is when you take the family out camping, they can't getaway and everyone knows, 'food just tastes better in the GREAT OUTDOORS'. This recipe is *My* way of cooking Carrots Delicious, from the *Love Creek Orchards* ADAMS APPLE COOKBOOK, Medina, Texas.

- The Chuckle Wagon Cooks
Steve & Jeanice Bias
La Marque, TX

Celtic Potatoes

12 inch Dutch oven - Serves 8 - 10

1 - 12 oz package bacon
8 cloves garlic, chopped
2 medium onions, chopped
8 lbs new red potatoes, quartered
2 Tbsp fresh dill chopped (reserve 1 Tbsp for garnish)
1 cup croutons (plain)
1 lb sharp Cheddar cheese, grated
1 lb white Cheddar cheese, grated
salt & pepper, to taste
Garnish:
        fresh green onion
        fresh dill, chopped
        dollop of sour cream

Sauté bacon till crisp, drain and set aside. Reserve 5 Tbsp bacon drippings in Dutch oven and sauté garlic and onions. Drop in potatoes and 1 Tbsp chopped dill. Cook till tender adding salt & pepper, to taste. Remove potatoes from heat and cool slightly. Add croutons and mix. Sprinkle all cheese on top then the crumbled bacon. Cover and bake in Dutch oven at approximately 350°F (10 coals on bottom and 12 - 14 coals on top) for 30 minutes or until cheese has completely melted. Remove from heat and garnish with green onions, dill and sour cream.

- Shem Ray, Jr. & Shem Ray, III
Sulphur Springs, TX

Chiles Rellenos

12 inch Dutch oven - Serves 8

1 - 7 oz can whole green chilies
2 Tbsp corn oil margarine
½ lb Monterey Jack cheese, grated
¼ lb Cheddar cheese, grated
6 egg whites, slightly beaten
1 Tbsp salt
1 cup biscuit mix
2 cups milk
1 Tbsp corn oil
2 Tbsp corn oil margarine

Preheat Dutch oven to 350°F with 9 charcoal briquets on bottom and 17 briquets on the top. Melt margarine in bottom of oven. Cut chilies into 1 inch wide strips and lay evenly over margarine. Combine the cheeses and spread evenly over chilies. Combine egg whites, corn oil, salt, biscuit mix and milk. Mix well using a wire whisk and pour over cheeses. Bake for 40 - 45 minutes until a light golden brown color.

- Cooking team of Wayne Switzer & Terry Elliot

Creamy Corn Delight

12 inch Dutch oven - Serves 8

3 - 16 oz pkgs. frozen yellow corn
1 - 8 oz cream cheese
¼ cup condensed milk

Place thawed frozen corn inside a 12 inch Dutch oven and cover with water, bring to a boil in oven then reduce heat and simmer for 5 minutes over 18 to 20 coals.

Pour off excess water then blend in the cream cheese over 9 or 10 coals until melted. Just before serving, fold in condensed milk a little at a time until well mixed.

- Wayne & Jay Switzer
Fort Worth, TX

Crunchy Sweet Potato Casserole

12 inch Dutch oven - Serves 8

3 cups sweet potatoes, cooked & mashed
1 stick margarine, melted
1 - 5 oz can evaporated milk
1 cup sugar
2 eggs, beaten
1 tsp vanilla
½ tsp nutmeg
1 tsp cinnamon
½ cup pecans, chopped
1 cup corn flakes, slightly crushed
½ cup brown sugar, firmly packed
1 stick margarine, melted

Mix well the first eight ingredients; pour into a 12 inch Dutch oven. Combine rest of ingredients spread evenly over potatoes.

Side Dishes

Bake at medium hot temperature (350°F) approximately 8 - 10 coals on bottom and 15 - 17 coals on top for thirty minutes or until top is golden brown.

- Alan & Joyce Switzer
Fort Worth, TX

German Green Bean Recipe

14 inch Dutch oven - Serves 6

2 - 16 oz cans French sliced green beans, drained (reserve liquid)
1 small can water chestnuts, sliced & drain
5 strips of bacon
1 large white onion, sliced
2 Tbsp flour
¾ cup drained green bean liquid
¼ cup cider vinegar
5 Tbsp sugar
1 tsp salt
¼ tsp pepper

Light 50 or more charcoal briquets. When coated with layer of white ash, place 12 briquets under Dutch oven.

Fry bacon till just crisp. Remove bacon. Sauté onion in bacon fat till translucent. Do not brown. Remove onion. Whisk flour into remaining bacon fat. Brown. Drain bean liquid into measuring cup (¾ cup). Discard remainder. Whisk bean liquid, vinegar, sugar, salt and pepper into flour and fat. Simmer till gravy consistency. Put drained beans, water chestnuts and onions into Dutch oven. Tear or chop bacon into ½ inch pieces, approximately, and add to oven. Mix completely. Put lid on Dutch oven.

Put 12 briquets on lid. Reduce briquets under oven to 10. You want the beans to simmer slowly. If they are cooking too fast,
German Green Bean Recipe continued.....

German Green Bean Recipe continued. . . . .
reduce coals one at a time till you get a slow simmer. Refrain from removing lid too often, as this reduces heat and extends cooking time. Replenish briquets under and over Dutch oven as they burn out. Simmer one hour. Great with any meat main dish.

Historical Note
This recipe is adapted from old recipes handed down in German families.

- The Prairie Kitchen
Cheryel Lemley
Midlothian, TX

Potatoes Italiano

10 inch Dutch oven

3 medium potatoes, peeled and quartered lengthwise
4 Tbsp oil   salt to taste
1 Tbsp rosemary   1 Tbsp sage

Over hot fire brown salted potatoes. Add sage evenly over potatoes and sprinkle rosemary on potatoes. Set pot off fire and cover. Use 8 briquets on pot lid and cook for about 30 minutes.

Note
This is so simple. You will not believe the results.

- The cooking team of Thomas Payne & Joe Williamson
Sulphur Springs, TX

Rice-A-Rancho

12 inch Dutch oven - Serves 10 - 12

4 Tbsp butter
1 medium onion, chopped
1 green pepper, chopped
1 orange or red bell pepper, chopped
4 cups Texmati® brown rice, uncooked
1 can stewed tomatoes, cut up
9 - 10 cups water or chicken broth (or any combination of the two)
2 tsp Fiesta® brand ground comino
2 tsp salt
1 tsp Adams® minced garlic
3+ Tbsp Pace® Picanté Sauce

With full fire (about 20 - 25 charcoal briquets) under a 12 inch Dutch oven sauté in butter the green pepper, orange or red pepper, and the onion until tender. Add rice and continue to sauté until rice is coated with butter and beginning to brown slightly. Cut up the stewed tomatoes (while still in the can is easiest) and add to the rice mixture. Stir. Add water/broth, spices, and picanté sauce. Stir to blend.

Place lid on the Dutch oven, cover with coals and bake/boil for approximately 30 minutes until rice is tender. Check near the end of the cooking time - it may be necessary to add extra water.

No extra garnish is needed as the orange and green peppers are so colorful!

Historical Note

This is a Prislovsky original recipe developed on our ranchó to feed our hungry niño and niña! Better than "Rice-a-Roni®" anytime!

- Mark & Pennie Prislovsky
Kerrville, TX

Spudz n' Cryan Applez

12 inch Dutch oven - Serves 12 - 16

½ lb bacon
12 large potatoes, peeled & sliced
6 large onions, peeled & sliced
½ lb butter
1 Tbsp salt (or more to taste)
½ Tbsp pepper (or more to taste)
1 can cream of mushroom soup
2 lbs mushrooms
1 cup sharp Cheddar cheese, shredded
cooking oil

Sauté cut up bacon in 12 inch oven until crisp. Add sliced potatoes and onions. Mix well together after adding salt and pepper. Add butter, cut up to melt easily through mixture. Stir regularly, every 5 to 10 minutes, to keep mixed and prevent burning. Add oil if necessary.

Cook for about 1 hour at 350°F - 375°F using 10 coals under and 14 - 16 on top. Remove bottom heat after 10 - 15 minutes and continue with top heat. Stop cooking when potatoes are done.

When almost done, pour cream of mushroom soup over top of potatoes. When done, sauté mushrooms in another pot or inverted lid. Cover potatoes with cheese and top with mushrooms. Then- mmm, serve to pleeze your palate.

Historical Note

Who knows where this idea originated, maybe with the ancient Romans. How many times have you baked or fried potatoes with some onions to enhance the flavor. This recipe just improves on everything!

- Larry & Bungy Hartshorn
Bandera, TX

Side Dishes

Texas Hominy Surprise

12 inch Dutch oven - Serves 4 - 6

2 - 16 oz cans white hominy
1 large white onion
½ cup water

1 lb bacon
1 large bell pepper
½ tsp seasoned salt

Cook bacon until crisp over a **full spread*** of charcoal briquets. Then remove from fire. Drain off excess grease. Dice or chop onion & pepper while bacon is cooling. Crumble bacon and mix with pepper and onion. Pour hominy with juice into pot, add onion/pepper mixture with ½ cup water. Put back on fire, bring to a boil and cook about 15 minutes. Season to taste

- Jeff Roberds
Midlothian, TX

*See 'The Dinwiddie Method of Charcoal Briquet' use on page 10.

Texas Trail Taters

14 inch Dutch oven - Serves 18 hungry cowpokes

1 lb bacon, sliced ¾ inch pieces
4 large onions, peeled & sliced
12 potatoes, cut into 1 inch chunks
salt & pepper
3 Tbsp Fiesta® Brisket Rub seasoning
4 carrots, sliced
1 small green pepper, chopped
1 small red pepper, chopped
1 yellow summer squash, sliced
1 zucchini squash, sliced
12 slices, white pasteurized cheese

Fry bacon until crisp, add onion and cook until transparent. Add
Texas Trail Taters continued. . . . .

Texas Trail Taters continued.....
potatoes, salt and pepper to taste, then add Fiesta® Brisket Rub seasoning. Add remaining vegetables so the zucchini and summer squash end up on top to provide moisture. Cook 30 - 40 minutes with 10 - 12 briquets on bottom and 15 - 17 on top (about 325°F - 350°F), stirring occasionally.

When potatoes and veggies are done, remove heat from bottom. Add slices of cheese on top, replace lid and cook until cheese melts.

Historical Note
At my very first Dutch oven cookoff in November of 1993, I was placed next to Dazel and Bill Ball and spent most of my time investigating the aroma from their pots. Dazel generously shared this recipe with me.

                   - From the cooking team of
                         Ike Craddock & Bill Spangler
                              Medina, TX

West Prong Potatoes
14 inch Dutch oven - Serves 6 - 8

6 Russet potatoes
½ cup Parmesan cheese
¾ tsp garlic powder
1½ tsp seasoned salt
6 Tbsp butter
1 can cream of celery soup
1 large onion, chopped
1½ cups fresh mushrooms, sliced
parsley flakes

Clean and peel potatoes, slice ¼ inch thick. Melt butter in Dutch oven and add onions and the entire can of cream of celery soup. Simmer ten minutes over **1 ring*** of charcoal briquets, then add potatoes, garlic powder, seasoned salt, mushrooms, cheese and sprinkle with parsley flakes. Bake with 6 coals on the bottom and 10

Side Dishes

coals on the top. Cook until potatoes pierce easily with a fork. Before serving sprinkle with 1 Tbsp of parmesan cheese and 1 Tbsp parsley flakes.

- The cooking team of
Don Cody & James Jones
Medina, TX

*See 'The Dinwiddie Method of Charcoal Briquet Use' on page 10.

Notes

Notes

Soup, Stew & Chili

B & B Chili

12 inch Dutch oven - Serves 10

2 lbs chili meat (brown & drain)
4 medium onion
2 large green bell peppers (chop & sauté in oil)

Add meat & 2 cans of Campbell's® Tomato Soup
2 cans ROTEL® Diced Tomatoes & Chilies
2 Tbsp chili powder
garlic to taste
season salt to taste
hickory smoke salt to taste
1 large jalapeno pepper (whole)

Simmer until done.

- Bud & Betty Burnette
San Antonio, TX

Chili Caliente

12 inch Dutch oven - Serves 4

1 lb ground beef
1 small onion, chopped
1 clove garlic, minced
2 Tbsp vegetable oil
1 - 6 oz can tomato paste
1¼ cups water
2 chili peppers
¼ tsp salt (optional)

optional ingredients:
   cayenne pepper
   meat tenderizer
   season salt
   additional peppers
   or anything else you
   can think of

In the bottom of the Dutch oven cook the onion, beef and garlic in the oil until the beef is browned. Next add all of the other ingredients except for the optional ones and all of the other spices. Bring to a boil and reduce some of the heat. Cover the Dutch oven and let simmer for about 30 minutes. Now, add all the desired optional ingredients and spices to taste. Cover the Dutch oven again and let simmer for another 10 minutes or more until the food is to your desired taste.

- Cooking team of
Stephen Dahlem & Chad Martichuski
Dallas, TX

Chicken Dumpling Stew

12 inch Dutch oven

1 whole chicken or 3 thick chicken breasts (We use skinless breasts to cut down on cholesterol.)
3 medium carrots   ¼ tsp cloves (optional)
3 large potatoes   1 tsp peppercorns
3 celery stalks   1 or 2 bay leaves
1 large onion
1 medium green pepper   ¼ tsp thyme or marjoram
1 cup corn or 1 - 8 oz can corn   2 tsp parsley, either fresh or
¾ cup mushrooms, sliced   dried
1 tsp salt (more may be added later to suit your taste)

Cut chicken breast into small cubes (1/2" to 3/4"). Using a 12 inch Dutch oven, boil chicken in 6 to 8 cup of water with peppercorns, salt and 2 slices of onion. (If chicken is an old hen, you may want to add a Tablespoon of vinegar to the water to help tenderize it.) Cook chicken for about 1 to 1½ hours in tightly covered Dutch oven, using 30 - 40 hot coals underneath.

Meanwhile, prepare vegetables. Clean and slice carrots, peel and dice potatoes, slice celery, dice remainder of onion and green pepper into large pieces. Clean mushrooms with a dry, soft cloth or brush and slice. Cut corn from cobs (or use canned corn). If using fresh parsley, mince several medium sized sprigs.

Chicken Dumpling Stew continued . . . . .

Chicken Dumpling Stew continued .....
(When chicken is done, you may want to skim off stock, if chicken breasts are fatty.)

Then add all prepared vegetables and all spices. Cook approximately 45 minutes, using the 30 - 40 hot coals underneath the oven.

While stew is cooking, prepare the dumpling mixture, using the following recipe suggestions.
- Biscuit mix or
- Use the dumpling recipe included with 'Old Fashioned Chicken and Dumplings' on page 71 of this book.

- Bill & Marilyn D'Lizarraga
Sulphur Springs, TX

Cowboy Stew

12 inch deep Dutch oven

30 charcoal briquets - start with 20 on the bottom then finish with 20 on the top and 10 on the bottom. Replace as needed.

1 Tbsp margarine
2 lbs ground meat
1 large onion, chopped
1 cup celery, chopped
1 clove garlic, chopped
¼ tsp sugar
1 can tomatoes
1 - 16 oz whole kernel corn
1 - 16 oz Ranch Style® beans
1 - 16 oz Ranch Style® beans with jalapenos
6 medium potatoes
4 - 5 carrots, sliced
4 cups water
salt & pepper to taste

Put oven over 20 briquets and brown meat and onions. After meat and onions are browned remove all but 10 briquets underneath the oven. Put remaining ingredients in oven and cook with 20 briquets on the lid, until potatoes and carrots are done. This recipe makes a full meal with a pan of cornbread.

- Wayne Switzer
Joshua, TX

L.S.D.O.S. Secret Ingredient Chili

(Fruit and Nut Chili)
14 inch Dutch oven - 8 main dish servings
16 side dish servings

Curry is just one of the surprising ingredients that flavors our L.S.D.O.S Secret Ingredient Chili. Other unexpected accents include apples, almonds, cocoa and a hint of cinnamon.

This chili is like our Lone Star Dutch Oven Society whose membership is made up from different and diverse personalities from all over the great Lone Star State.

Stir up a batch and see what you think!
By the way the *secret ingredient* in the Lone Star Dutch Oven Society are love of good food, friends, fun and family.

1½ lbs lean ground beef
4 medium onions, chopped (2 cups)
3 cloves garlic, minced
2 - 16 oz can tomatoes, cut up
1 - 15 oz can tomato sauce
1 - 14½ oz can chicken broth
3 medium green, red, or yellow sweet peppers,
       chopped (2¼ cups)
2 - 4 oz cans diced green chili peppers, drained
2 cooking apples, cored & chopped
L.S.D.O.S. Secret Ingredient Chili continued. . . .

L.S.D.O.S. Secret Ingredient Chili continued. . . .
3 Tbsp chili powder
2 Tbsp unsweetened cocoa powder
1 Tbsp curry powder
1 tsp ground cinnamon
1 - 15 oz can red kidney beans, drained & rinsed
2/3 cup almonds, slivered
optional:
Top with raisins, sour cream, Cheddar cheese or plain yogurt

In 14 inch Dutch oven cook beef, onions, garlic until meat is brown, 24 briquets on the bottom. Drain off fat. Stir in undrained tomatoes, tomato sauce, broth, peppers, green chili peppers, apples, chili powder, cocoa, curry powder and cinnamon. Bring to a boil with 24 briquets on the bottom. Cover and reduce heat to a simmer for 1 hour. Add 14 new briquets on the bottom and 14 on the top. Add kidney beans and almonds. Heat through.

Serve with raisins, sour cream, Cheddar cheese, or yogurt, if desired.

- The Chuckle Wagon Cookers
Steve & Jeanice Bias
La Marque, TX

Quick Breads

Aunt Mae's Peach Muffins

14 inch Dutch oven with foil cups - Yields 12 muffins

1½ cups all purpose flour
½ cup salad oil
¾ tsp salt
1¼ cups fresh peaches, coarsely chopped
½ tsp baking soda
½ tsp vanilla
1 cup sugar
1/8 tsp almond extract
2 eggs, well beaten
½ cup almonds, chopped

Combine flour, salt, baking soda and sugar. Make a well in center of dry ingredients. Add eggs and oil. Lightly stir only until dry ingredients are moistened. Lightly stir in peaches, vanilla, almond extract and almonds. Fill cups 2/3 full with batter. Place foil muffin cups in preheated 14 inch Dutch oven. Cook using 4 coals on bottom and 20 coals on top, for 20 - 25 minutes, or until muffins test done. For peach bread, spoon batter into 10 inch greased preheated Dutch oven. Cook with 3 coals on bottom and 12 coals on top for 1 hour or until bread tests done.

Historical Note

I was in the supermarket not long ago and saw summer's first peaches. At once my mind raced back to Falfurrias, Texas and Aunt Mae's peach muffins. I know she made them especially for all the kids that would visit her little farm on weekends. She would have each of the kids pick a small basket-full and bring them back to the back, screened porch. There we would "help" peel and slice, until we had enough for a cobbler and several dozen muffins. When it was time for good-byes, each of the kids would get a couple of muffins, wrapped in brown paper, for the trip home.

- James D. Cook
Corpus Christi, TX

Chunky Pecan Muffins

12 inch Dutch oven - Yields 12 muffins

1½ cups all purpose flour
2 tsp baking powder
¼ tsp salt
½ cup brown sugar, firmly packed
pinch of allspice
1 egg, slightly beaten
1/3 cup milk
¼ cup maple flavored syrup
½ cup butter or margarine, melted
1 cup pecans, coarsely chopped
1 tsp vanilla
¼ cup sugar
¼ tsp cinnamon
¼ cup butter or margarine, melted

Combine first 5 ingredients in a medium bowl; making a well in the center of the mixture.

Combine egg, milk, syrup, and ½ cup butter; add to dry ingredients, stirring just until moistened. Stir in pecans and vanilla. Fill foil muffin cups 2/3rds full and place in Dutch oven.

Place 8 coals on top and 14 coals on bottom.

Bake for 15 to 20 minutes.

Combine sugar and cinnamon. Dip tops of warm muffins in remaining ¼ cup butter, then into cinnamon sugar mixture.

- Exploradors Dutch Oven Team
Bill & Cindy Williamson
Allen, TX

Cindy's Cornbread Crumble

14 inch Dutch oven - Serves 6 - 8

1 cup cornmeal
1 cup flour
4 tsp baking powder
½ tsp salt
1 egg
1 cup milk
¼ cup oil

Put oil in oven and heat. Combine first six ingredients and blend lightly together until all ingredients are just moist. Pour mixture over heated oil.

Put 8 charcoal briquets on bottom and 16 on top of Dutch oven. Cook 20 - 25 minutes and let cool.

While cornbread cools, fry bacon on lid and crumble onto cornbread.

Combine:
    5 green onions, chopped
    1 cup Hellmans® mayonnaise
    1 bell pepper, chopped
    1 tomato, chopped

Mix all ingredients and serve with cornbread.

Country Creole Corn Bread

14 inch Dutch oven - Yields 14 servings

2 cups cooked rice
1½ cups yellow cornmeal
1 cup onion, chopped
1 to 2 Tbsp jalapeno peppers, seeded & chopped
1 tsp salt
½ tsp baking soda
3 eggs
1½ cups milk
1/3 cup vegetable oil
1 - 12 oz can cream style corn
3 cups (12 oz) Cheddar cheese, shredded
1 to 1½ lbs ground meat, sausage or shrimp
shrimp boil

In a large bowl, combine rice, cornmeal, onion, peppers, salt and baking soda. In another bowl, beat eggs, milk and oil. Add corn and mix well. Stir into rice mixture until blended. Add ground meat or sausage that has been browned or shrimp that has been about half cooked in shrimp boil. Fold in cheese.

Sprinkle a well greased 14 inch Dutch oven with cornmeal. Pour batter into a preheated Dutch oven. Cook with 14 coals on bottom and 20 coals on top for 20 - 30 minutes, then remove from coals and cook only from the top for 15 - 20 minutes or until done.

- Paul & Sissy Garrison
Medina, TX

Dutch Oven Biscuits

12 inch Dutch oven - Feeds 8 - 10 people

4 cups all purpose flour
2 Tbsp Rumford® baking soda
1 tsp salt
1 cup butter (2 sticks)
1½ cups milk

Sift together flour, baking powder and salt. Cut in butter with a pastry blender or 2 knives until mixture has the texture of coarse meal. Add milk and stir just until dough is mixed. This should be a very soft dough. Knead 3 or 4 times until dough is mixed and holds together well.

On a well floured flat surface roll or pat out to ½ inch to ¼ inch thickness. Cut with a floured biscuit cutter. Preheat Dutch oven and lid to about 425°F, with 21 coals on top and 10 on the bottom. Grease oven and place biscuits close together. Cover and bake for 10 - 15 minutes with twice as many coals on top as on the bottom. Be careful not to burn the bottoms - remember the oven is going to be very hot.

Biscuits are done when the tops are golden brown. Brush tops with melted butter and serve warm. Remember that if left to cool in a Dutch oven most breads will become soggy on the bottom; so it is best to serve the biscuits hot out of the pan, or place them on a wire rack to cool.

Historical Note
This is an old recipe that can be found in James Beard's *Beard on Bread* cookbook.

- The Hatfield Ranch Cocineros
Dan Hatfield & Cindy Rather
Medina, TX

Dutch Oven Cornbread

12 inch Dutch oven - Yields 8 - 10 servings

2½ cups all purpose flour	2 cups milk
1½ cups cornmeal	½ cup vegetable oil or margarine
½ cup sugar	2 eggs, beaten
4 tsp baking powder	1 large onion, minced
1 tsp salt	1 - 10 oz can whole kernel corn

Preheat oven by making a ring of coals a little bigger than the bottom of the Dutch oven. Place approximately 8 - 10 coals on lid after heating the oven, grease with shortening.

Combine dry ingredients.

Stir in milk, oil and eggs, mixing just until the dry ingredients are moist.

Add onion and drained whole kernel corn.

Pour into Dutch oven.

Bake 20 - 25 minutes or until golden brown and knife inserted near the center comes out clean.

Serve warm with lots of butter.

- Audra Sanders
Seabrook, TX

Granny Lemley's Cheese Biscuits

14 inch Dutch oven - Feeds 8 - 10 people

4 cups unbleached flour, sifted
2 Tbsp baking powder
1 tsp salt
1 cup Cheddar cheese, grated
1 cup lard or butter
1½ cups milk

Combine flour, baking powder and salt. Fold in cheese, thoroughly coating cheese with flour mixture. Mix in softened lard or butter. Add milk and stir just until dough is mixed. Knead 3 or 4 time on lightly floured board. Pat out to ½ inch thickness, cut biscuits with floured biscuit cutter.

Preheat Dutch oven and lid to about 425°F, with approximately 13 coals on top and bottom. Grease oven and place biscuits in oven, spacing evenly. Cover and bake for 10 - 15 minutes. Be careful not to burn the bottoms. Give the oven a quarter turn every few minutes turning the lid in the opposite direction. Try not to open the lid.

Biscuits are done when the tops are golden brown. Brush tops with melted butter and serve warm. It is best to serve biscuits hot out of the oven, or remove them to a plate to cool because if left to cool in the oven they will become soggy on the bottom.

Variation:
Herb Cheese Biscuits: Add 1 tsp poultry seasoning or any combination of your favorite herbs such as caraway, dill, oregano, cardamom or marjoram to the flour mixture. Fresh herbs of course are best.

Historical Note
This recipe was adapted from Granny's wood stove recipe.

- The Prairie Kitchen
Cheryel Lemley
Covington, TX

Jeanice's Breakfast Biscuits

14 inch Dutch oven - Yields 36 biscuits
34 mesquite charcoal briquets

5 cups flour
2 cups brown sugar
1 cup buttermilk
2 tsp butter, melted
2 eggs
36 small smoked sausages

½ cup black walnuts
½ cup dried apples
1 tsp vanilla
½ tsp baking powder
1 tsp baking soda

- Mix together well the sugar, vanilla and eggs.
- Add baking soda to buttermilk.
- Sift flour and baking powder together.
- Add 3 cups of flour mixture to egg/sugar mixture, alternately with buttermilk.
- Add nuts, apples and butter.
- Work in the rest of the flour.
- Pull dough off in 1 inch balls and roll or pat out to 1/4 inch thick.
- Place one of the sausages on the dough, fold over and seal.
- Arrange biscuits in a 14 inch Dutch oven and bake at 350°F by using 21 briquets on the top of the oven and 11 briquets on the bottom. Bake for 30 minutes or until brown.

Note

If'n your the one doing the cookin, grab a couple fir yourself before theys all gone!

- The Chuckle Wagon Cookers
Steve & Jeanice Bias
La Marque, TX

Pan de Campo (Camp Bread)
12 inch Dutch oven - Serves 8 - 10

2 cups flour	1 tsp sugar
2 tsp baking powder	1/3 cup cooking oil
1 tsp salt	½ cup cold milk

Preheat oven with 10 briquets on the bottom and 20 on the top. Combine all the ingredients. Be careful when kneading the dough not to over knead it, if dough is over worked it becomes tough. If dough feels dry, add a few drops of milk. Form dough into ½ inch thick circle to fit the oven.

Place in heated oven. With a fork pierce the dough in order to allow the steam to escape.

Bake for 10 - 15 minutes.
- Elliot Switzer

Pan de Campo (Camp Bread)
10 - 12 inch cast iron skillet

2 cups flour	1 cup milk
1 tsp salt	2 Tbsp oil
2 tsp baking powder	

Mix dry ingredients. Add oil and milk. Roll out 3/4 inch thick like biscuit dough. Preheat covered skillet for 5 minutes over medium low heat. Put in dough and spread out to cover bottom of a 10 - 12 inch skillet. Cover and bake 6 or 7 minutes. Turn the dough over and bake 5 minutes more.
- Lee Fisher
Austin, TX

Quick Breads

Poor Charlie's Sourdough Cornbread
14 inch Dutch oven - Serves 8

1 cup sourdough starter
2 cups cornmeal (enough to make a batter)
1½ cups milk
2 Tbsp sugar
2 eggs, beaten
¼ cup butter or fat (melted & still warm)
2 pinches salt
2 pinches baking soda

Mix starter, cornmeal, milk, eggs and stir thoroughly in a large bowl. Stir in melted butter, salt and baking soda. Turn into a greased 14 inch Dutch oven. Place oven over 15 - 20 coals and place 15 - 20 coals on the lid. Bake for 25 - 30 minutes.

- Todd & Sissie Sandidge
Bandera, TX

Sourdough Biscuits
12 inch Dutch oven - Yields 4 servings

1 cup sourdough starter
2½ cups flour
1 cup milk
1 tsp salt
1 tsp baking soda
1 Tbsp brown sugar
1 Tbsp lard (salt pork, butter, or oil can be substituted)
melted bacon fat

Mix starter, flour and milk into a stiff dough. Cover and place in a warm place for 45 minutes to 8 hours to rise.

Sourdough Biscuits continued. . . . .

Sourdough Biscuits continued. . . . .

When ready to bake, combine salt, soda and sugar. Melt the lard and mix all into the risen dough. Knead thoroughly. Break off dough the size of an egg and roll in melted bacon fat, including the sides, top and bottom. Place each piece in a biscuit pan.

Preheat and pre-grease Dutch oven and lid. Place the biscuit pan on pebbles in the Dutch oven to allow air to circulate beneath it. Bake at 350°F with 18 coals on the top and 10 coals underneath for 20 - 30 minutes.

       - Los Cocineros de Arroyo Seco
        Carl Hacker & Claudia Kozinetz
          Houston, TX

Notes

Yeast Breads

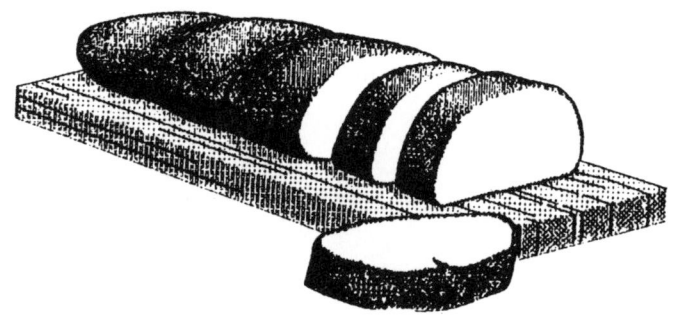

Angel Biscuits

12 inch Dutch oven
29 charcoal briquets (19 top/10 bottom)

2½ cups flour
6 Tbsp liquid shortening
1½ tsp baking powder
½ tsp baking soda
½ tsp salt
1½ tsp yeast (1 pkg.)
¼ cup warm water (100°F - 115°F)
1 cup buttermilk
1½ Tbsp sugar

Warm Dutch oven & lid, then set aside without briquets but with the lid on to hold in the heat.
Mix dry ingredients with liquid shortening.
Dissolve yeast in warm water, stir into buttermilk.
Add buttermilk to dry ingredients mixture & mix all together in a bowl.
Set bowl into oven or a warm place to rise for about 15 minutes.
Up end bowl onto lightly floured surface, roll or pat dough down to approximately 1 - 1½ inches thick, cut into biscuits.
Lightly grease inside of oven.
Put biscuits into oven, return oven to briquets, top & bottom, and bake covered for 12 - 14 minutes or until done.
Serve & enjoy!

- From the 2 B's Dutch Oven team of
Bill & Beverly Brummel
San Antonio, TX

Yeast Bread

Apple Roly Polys

12 inch Dutch oven - Serves 8 - 10

Dough:
2 Tbsp instant yeast
½ cup warm water (105°F - 115°F)
1¼ cups buttermilk
2 eggs
5½ to 6 cups whole wheat flour (may use all-purpose flour or a combination)
½ cup butter, softened
½ cup honey
2 tsp baking powder
2 tsp salt

Filling:
2 Tbsp butter, melted
1 cup brown sugar
cinnamon
3 to 4 cups apples, grated
1 cup pecans, chopped

Icing:
½ cup confectioner's sugar
½ Tbsp milk
½ tsp vanilla

In a large bowl, dissolve yeast in warm water. Add buttermilk, eggs, 2½ cups flour, butter, sugar, baking powder, and salt. Blend ½ minute with a hand cranked beater or beat with a spoon, scraping bowl often. Beat 2 minutes more. Stir in enough remaining flour to make dough easy to handle. (Dough should remain soft and slightly sticky.)

Turn dough onto a well-floured board. Knead 5 minutes or about 200 turns. Roll out into large rectangle (15" x 9"); spread with butter. Cover with brown sugar. Shake a heavy coating of cinnamon over all. Sprinkle on grated apples and pecans. Roll up, beginning at wide side. Pinch edge of dough into roll to seal well. Cut roll into even slices (dental floss works well!) Place right up next to each other in an oiled 12 inch Dutch oven. Put the lid on and
Apple Roly Polys continued. . . . .

Apple Roly Polys continued. . . . .
place in a warm place to rise until not quite double (about 1 hour).

Bake with 9 coals on bottom and 15 coals on the top for 25 to 30 minutes.

Prepare icing: mix icing ingredients in a small bowl until smooth. While warm, drizzle frosting over rolls.

Historical Note

This recipe was developed for the '95 Cookoff. You will need to stand clear of the stampede when serving if your family loves sweet rolls like ours does!

- Mark & Pennie Prislovsky
Kerrville, TX

Autumn Grape Cluster
16 inch Dutch oven - Feeds 8 to 10 people

1 Tbsp yeast	3 cups bread flour
1/4 cup warm water	1 cup warm milk
1/8 tsp sugar	1 Tbsp butter, softened
1 tsp salt	1 egg yolk
1 Tbsp sugar	1 tsp water

Mix dry yeast in water, sprinkle the 1/8 tsp sugar over the yeast mixture to activate. Mix milk, butter, salt and 1 Tbsp sugar well. Add ½ amount of flour, mix thoroughly. Add yeast mixture, stir well, then add the rest of the flour (retaining ½ cup). The dough will be stiff. Sprinkle some of the remaining flour on a flat surface. Knead until dough is smooth. Place dough in a greased bowl, cover and let rise until double in bulk (approximately 1 hour).

Yeast Bread

Punch dough down. Grease your Dutch oven. To shape a grape cluster: Using kitchen scissors, snip the dough into pieces, varying the sizes slightly. Set 4 to 6 small pieces aside. To form the grapes, roll remaining pieces into balls. With your finger, rub each ball with a little water as you assemble them together into a grape cluster in the Dutch oven. Start with 7 or 8 balls at the top of the cluster and continuing in loosely organized rows, end with 1 ball at the bottom of the cluster. Add a layer of balls on top of these. Shape the reserved small pieces of dough into leaves, a stem and a curly vine. With a knife mark veins in the leaves, if desired. When finished let rise in a warm place for about 15 minutes.

In a small bowl combine egg yolk and water. Brush grape cluster with egg wash. Place the Dutch oven on one or two shovels* of hot coals and also put a shovel of coals on the top of the lid. Bake approximately 10 - 15 minutes. Remove Dutch oven from coals and continue baking with coals on the top for approximately 10 - 15 minutes or until the cluster is golden brown and sounds hollow when thumped. Carefully remove the pan and cool on a wire rack.
(*Small coal or camping shovel)

Historical Note

This recipe is a combination of a couple of different recipes. The idea was created when Cindy Rather was searching through a *Better Homes and Gardens* book one day and came across an article on winning bread recipes. I then combined the style of bread with a Dutch oven roll recipe by Juanita Kohler. This is a showy bread for fun or special occasions.

                       - From the Hatfield Ranch Cocineros
                            Dan Hatfield & Cindy Rather
                                   Medina, TX

Cinnamon Breakfast Rolls
12 inch Dutch oven - Serves 12 - 16

2½ Tbsp warm water	1 Tbsp sugar
1 pkg. dry active yeast	2½ cups self-rising flour
1 tsp baking soda	½ cup shortening
1 cup buttermilk	4 Tbsp butter, melted
1/3 cup sugar	1 tsp cinnamon

½ cup raisins, softened in warm water & drained
½ cup pecans, chopped

Dissolve sugar in warm water, add in yeast and mix. Set aside until yeast blooms.

In bowl, mix flour and baking soda. Cut-in shortening with a pastry blender until all is crumbly and not large lumps. Add yeast mixture and stir in with buttermilk until well blended. Make a ball of the dough, cover and let rise some.

When ready, knead dough slightly on a floured board while forming an oblong shape. Roll to about 8" x 18". Combine sugar with cinnamon, pecans and raisins. Brush melted butter over dough, then spread sugar mixture over entire surface. From long side of dough, roll up, jelly-roll fashion. Cut into 16 slices and place flat side down in an oiled Dutch oven. Bake about 20 minutes or until nicely browned and toothpick inserted comes out clean. Keep oven hot, 375°F - 400°F, by placing 8 - 10 briquets under and 16 -18 briquets over. After 8 - 10 minutes remove bottom heat and continue with top heat.

Glaze:
1 cup powdered sugar,   1 - 2 Tbsp milk,   ¼ tsp vanilla.
Combine sugar, vanilla and small amount of milk. Blend until smooth and just pourable by gradually adding milk. Pour over hot rolls when done and let cool some before serving.

Note
These rolls are just plain good, particularly when accompanied with a hot cup of black coffee.

- Larry & Bungy Hartshorn
Bandera, TX

Cinnamon Rolls

12 inch Dutch oven - Serves 12

1 pkg. dry active yeast
¼ cup warm water
1/8 tsp sugar
1 tsp salt
1 Tbsp sugar
3 cups bread flour
1 cup milk, warm
1 Tbsp butter

Mix dry yeast in warm water, sprinkle the 1/8 tsp sugar over the yeast mixture to activate. Mix milk, butter, salt and sugar, stir well. Add one-half amount of flour, mix thoroughly. Add yeast mixture, stir well, then add the rest of the flour (retaining one-half cup). The dough will be stiff. Sprinkle some of the remaining flour on a flat surface. Knead until dough is smooth. Form dough into smooth rolls and place into greased 12 inch Dutch oven. Cover and let rise until double in bulk. Place Dutch oven on 15 coals and place 20 - 25 coals on top of lid. Bake approximately 10 - 15 minutes from top and bottom. Remove Dutch oven from coals and continue baking with coals on top for approximately 10 - 15 minutes or until rolls are golden brown.

Variation:
Cinnamon Rolls: Brown sugar, cinnamon, raisins or nuts as desired. Roll dough in a flat rectangle shape (approximately ¼ inch thick). Spread or sprinkle the filling on the rolled dough. Roll up and pinch edges together. Cut into 1 inch slices and place in greased 12 inch Dutch oven, edges touching. Let rise until double in bulk. Bake in the same manner as the Dutch oven rolls.

- Paul & Sissy Garrison
Medina, TX

Cinnamon Surprise Rolls

14 inch Dutch oven

Dough:

1 pkg. dry yeast	6 or more cups flour
1 cup warm water	½ tsp salt
¾ cup vegetable oil	½ tsp baking soda
¾ cup sugar	3 Tbsp baking powder
2 cups buttermilk	

Dissolve yeast in hot water. Add oil, sugar and buttermilk. Sift flour with salt, baking soda, and baking powder and add to liquid mixture. Knead in more flour until dough is smooth. Let rise. Roll out into rectangle shape ¼ to ½ inch thick.

Filling:
Mix the following ingredients together:
1 cup brown sugar
1 - 3¾ oz pkg. regular butterscotch pudding mix
¼ cup granulated sugar
1 tsp cinnamon
½ tsp cloves
¼ tsp ginger
½ cup chopped pecans

½ cup butter, melted

Grease and flour Dutch oven. Sprinkle a light layer of spice mixture on bottom of Dutch oven. Brush rolled dough with some of the melted butter. Sprinkle remaining spice mixture over dough. Roll up like a jelly roll. Cut into 1" thick slices and place cut side down in Dutch oven. Pour remaining melted butter over top of dough. Let rise until double in size. Bake at 350°F for 30 - 45 minutes (10 - 12 coals on bottom and 16 - 18 coals on top). Let sit in pan 10 - 15 minutes before turning over to serve.

- Cooking team of
Ike Craddock & Bill Spangler
Medina, TX

Cream Cheese 'n Apple Rolls

12 inch Dutch oven - Serves 12 - 16

2½ Tbsp warm water	1 Tbsp sugar
1 pkg. dry active yeast	2½ cups self-rising flour
1 tsp baking soda	½ cup shortening
1 cup buttermilk	4 oz cream cheese, softened
1/3 cup apple butter	½ cup brown sugar, packed
1½ cups powdered sugar	2½ Tbsp apple juice

Dissolve sugar in warm water, add in yeast and mix. Set aside until yeast blooms.

In bowl, mix flour and baking soda. Cut-in shortening with a pastry blender until all is crumbly and no large lumps. Add yeast mixture and stir in with buttermilk until well blended. Make a ball of the dough, cover and let rise some.

When ready, knead dough slightly on a floured board while forming an oblong shape. Roll to about 10" x 16".

In a bowl, combine apple butter, softened cream cheese and brown sugar. Beat until smooth. Spread evenly over dough. Roll from long side like a jelly-roll. Cut 1 inch slices and place flat side down in a oiled Dutch oven. Bake about 20 minutes or until rolls are nicely browned and an inserted toothpick comes out clean.

Glaze:

Mix powdered sugar and apple juice in bowl until smooth and just pourable. Pour over hot rolls.

Note

Something different and a nice finish to a light meal, not overwhelming.

- Larry & Bungy Hartshorn
Bandera, TX

Dinner Rolls

14 inch Dutch oven - Serves 8 - 16

2 cups warm water
2 pkgs. rapid rise yeast
3 Tbsp sugar
7 cups bread flour
2 tsp salt

½ cup powdered milk
2 Tbsp butter, melted
2 eggs, beaten
extra flour for kneading
1 stick cold butter

- Stir yeast and sugar into warm water. Let it sit for 10 minutes until foamy.
- Combine flour, salt, and powdered milk in a large mixing bowl.
- When yeast water has finished the 10 minutes of activation time, combine with melted butter and eggs. Add this to the dry ingredients and mix into a dough.
- Knead dough for 3 minutes, adding extra flour as needed for easier handling.
- Place dough into a large, oiled bowl or Dutch oven, turning it once to oil top of dough.
- Cover with a towel or lid and put in a warm, draft-free place. Allow dough to rise until doubled in size, 30 minutes to 1 hour, depending on the temperature.
- When dough is doubled, punch it down, turn out onto a floured surface, and knead for 2 minutes more.
- Cut dough into 20 equal pieces; cut dough in half, then cut those 2 sections in half again, then cut those 4 sections into fifths.
- Form dough into round balls and place evenly into a well oiled 14 inch Dutch oven.
- Place lid on oven and allow dough to rise until almost doubled. About 15 minutes into this rise, light enough charcoal for **3 & ½ rings***.
- When dough balls have risen, place oven over **1 ring*** of freshly lit charcoal and place **1 & ½ rings*** on lid.
- Bake 25 minutes, giving oven a 1/3 turn every 8 minutes (turn more often if it's windy).
- If necessary, add a **full spread*** to lid until rolls are golden brown (2 - 3 minutes) and peek often.
- Take oven off coals and remove coals from lid.
- Glaze rolls by rubbing them with a stick of cold butter.

Yeast Bread

- Loosen the sides of the rolls from the oven, shake the oven sharply up and down to loosen them from the bottom, and turn them out onto a towel. Then turn them back onto the inverted Dutch oven lid for serving.

- Dos Dinwiddies
Duane & Sandy Dinwiddie
Houston, TX

*See 'The Dinwiddie Method of Charcoal Briquet Use' on page 10.

Dutch Oven Rolls

14 inch Dutch oven - Yield about 24 rolls

2 Tbsp yeast	2 Tbsp sugar
½ cup warm water	6 cups flour
¼ tsp sugar	2 cups warm milk
2 tsp salt	2 Tbsp butter

Mix dry yeast in water, sprinkle the ¼ tsp sugar over the yeast mixture to activate. Mix milk, butter, salt and sugar, stir well. Add one-half amount of flour, mix thoroughly. Add yeast mixture, stir well, then add the rest of the flour (retaining ½ to 1 cup). The dough will be stiff. Sprinkle some of the remaining flour on a flat surface. Knead until dough is smooth. Place dough in greased bowl, cover and let rise until double in bulk (approximately 1 hour). Shape dough into smooth rolls and place in greased Dutch oven. Cover and let rise until double in bulk. Place the Dutch oven on one or two shovels of hot coals and also put a shovel of coals on the top of the lid.

Bake approximately 10 - 15 minutes from top and bottom. Remove Dutch oven from coals and continue baking with coals on top for approximately 10 - 15 minutes or until rolls are golden brown.

Dutch Oven Rolls continued . . .

Dutch Oven Rolls continued . . . .
Variations:
Cinnamon Rolls: Butter, brown sugar, white sugar, cinnamon and nuts or raisins as desired.

Roll dough in a flat rectangle shape (approximately ¼ inch thick). Brush melted butter on dough then add remaining ingredients. Roll up like a jelly roll and cut into 1 inch thick slices. Place in greased Dutch oven, edges touching. Let rise until double in bulk. Bake in the same manner as the Dutch oven rolls.

Historical Notes
This is a recipe that I came across in the *World Championship Dutch Oven Cookbook*. It is Juanita Kohler's recipe and it has always worked great for me.

\- From the Hatfield Ranch Cocineros
Dan Hatfield & Cindy Rather
Medina, TX

Dutch Oven Sourdough Rolls
16 inch Dutch oven

3 cups warm water
2 pkgs. dry yeast (2 Tbsp)
8 cups unsifted flour
4 tsp salt
2 cups additional unsifted flour
2 cups sourdough starter
4 tsp sugar
1 Tbsp baking soda

Add warm water and yeast. Add sourdough starter, 8 cups flour and the sugar. Blend well. Cover and put in a warm place (until double in volume, about 2 hours). Mix soda, salt and 2 cups of flour. Stir well and add to other mixture. Turn out on a floured board and knead until smooth. Shape into rolls, place in a greased 16 inch

Yeast Bread

Dutch oven. When double in bulk, bake from the top and bottom on a medium fire for approximately 10 - 15 minutes. (Use 12 - 14 coals on the bottom and 18 - 20 coals on the top.) Remove Dutch oven from the coals and continue to bake with coals on lid for an additional 15 - 20 minutes or until golden brown. The rolls will sound hollow when thumped with a finger. Brush tops with melted butter before serving.

Historical Note

This recipe was adapted from a recipe in the *World Championship Dutch Oven Cookbook.*

- From the cooking team of
Ike Craddock & Bill Spangler
Medina, TX

Grandma's Icebox Hot Rolls

12 inch Dutch oven - Serves 8

1 quart sweet milk
2 cakes yeast
2/3 cup water
1 cup sugar
oil

½ cup shortening
4 tsp salt
2 eggs
9 cups flour (approximately)

The night before:
- Over low heat warm water to dissolve yeast then set aside.
- Slowly warm milk to the touch.
- Melt shortening and add to the warm milk.
- Add yeast mixture.
- In a large bowl stir together the warm milk mixture with sugar and eggs.
- Add salt to your first cup of flour and begin stirring in the flour a cup full at a time.
- When you have a soft dough turn out onto a floured table. Fold the flour into the dough only about 4 or 5 times. Oil a large bowl and lift dough into bowl.

Dutch Oven Rolls continued . . . . .

Lone Star Dutch Oven Society Cookbook

Dutch Oven Rolls continued . . . .
- Flip the dough so all sides will be oiled. Cover the bowl.
- SET INTO ICEBOX (refrigerator) OVERNIGHT TO RISE.

The next morning:
Turn dough out onto floured table and fold 4 or 5 times again. Pinch off handfuls of dough and place in a well greased, slightly warm Dutch oven. Set aside in a warm place to rise. When rolls have risen, place over **1 ring*** of coals with **1½ rings*** of coals on the lid. Bake for 30 to 40 minutes. Replace coals as needed.

Historical Note

This recipe has been bringing mother-in-law and daughter-in-law together in my husband's family for generations.

This is a touch and feel recipe. Just having the list of ingredients does not produce a good batch of hot rolls. You must be taught to feel the warmth of the yeast, water, milk and shortening. A tea cup is always used to measure out the flour (along with a cup of tea while you work).

Kneading the dough is another art handed down. Not too much but gently folding like a bath towel. Too much kneading and your rolls could be used to build a fireplace hearth.

After the dough is prepared it is set in the *icebox* (refrigerator to you young'ens) to rise over night. This is usually done on Saturday night so the dough will be ready to shape into rolls the next morning.

The melt in your mouth yeast rolls are a dinner delight and have graced out Sunday and holiday dinner tables for generations.

> \- Cherokee Chefs
> Bonita & Felicia Sanders
> Seabrook, TX

*See 'The Dinwiddie Method of Charcoal Briquet Use' on page 10.

Home Style White Bread
12 inch Dutch oven - Serves 6

1 pkg. dry yeast
1 cup warm water (105° - 115°F)
1 Tbsp sugar
2 Tbsp shortening
1 egg
¼ tsp salt
3 to 3½ cups all-purpose flour

Dissolve yeast in warm water in a large mixing bowl, let stand 5 minutes. Add sugar, shortening, egg, salt and half of the flour. Fold together until smooth. Gradually stir in enough remaining flour to make a soft dough.

Place dough in a well-greased bowl, turning to grease top. Cover and let rise in a warm place (about 85°F), free from drafts, 1 hour or until doubled in bulk.

Punch dough down, turn out onto a lightly floured surface, and knead 4 or 5 times. Shape and bake 45 minutes in a medium hot Dutch oven or until golden brown.

Instructions for medium hot Dutch oven (350°F):
25 charcoal briquets - Place 2/3 of coals on top of Dutch oven and 1/3 coals on the bottom of the Dutch oven.

- Alan & Wayne Switzer
Fort Worth, TX

Marie Crowe's Bread

14 inch Dutch oven - Yields 36 to 48 rolls or 4 small loaf pans

3 cups lukewarm water	2 pkgs. dry, active, yeast
½ cup sugar	7 cups flour
2/3 cup shortening, softened	1 egg
1½ tsp salt	

Dissolve yeast in ½ cup water.
In a large bowl add remaining water, shortening, salt, egg, yeast.
Mix add flour gradually until the batter becomes stiff.
Pour onto floured board and work until easily handled.
Put into large, well oiled pan, let rise until double in size.
Set up Dutch oven; 21 charcoal briquets on top, and 11 on the bottom, (350°F).
Bake for 30 minutes then remove the oven from the bottom heat.
Bake with top heat only, 10 minutes more or until top of bread is golden brown.
Brush with butter. (Bake at home for 25 - 30 minutes at 350°F.)

Serve warm

Historical Note

Mrs. Crowe lived in Cassville, Missouri where her son now runs the family restaurant. The Crowe Restaurant is known for her bread recipe. Little does her son Jerry know that Jeanice and Marie did some recipe trading.

- The Chuckle Wagon Cookers
Steve & Jeanice Bias
La Marque, TX

Yeast Bread

Ranch Rolls

12 inch Dutch oven - Serves 6 - 8

1 Tbsp dry yeast
¼ cup warm water
1/8 tsp sugar
1 Tsp salt
1 Tbsp sugar

1 egg
3½ cups flour
1 cup warm milk
1½ Tbsp butter

Mix yeast in water, sprinkle 1/8 tsp sugar over yeast mixture to activate. Mix milk, butter, salt, sugar and egg, stir well. Add 1½ cups flour and mix thoroughly. Add yeast mixture, stir well, then add another 1½ cups flour mix and knead. Mix the ½ cup of flour as needed to keep dough from sticking. Put dough in bowl or lightly oiled Dutch oven, cover and let rise until dough doubles. After it has risen break off into small rolls and put into Dutch oven. Cover and let rolls rise until rolls double in size. Bake with approximately 6 coals on the bottom and 15 coals on the top for 15 minutes. Remove oven from bottom heat and continue to cook with top heat only.

- Don Cody & James Jones
Medina, TX

Rancher's Sourdough Rolls

14 inch Dutch oven - Serves 7 - 8

1 pkg. yeast
1/3 cup sugar
1½ cups warm water
5 cups flour
3 Tbsp cooking oil
1 cup sourdough starter
2 tsp salt
½ stick butter, melted

Rancher's Sourdough Rolls continue . . . . .

Rancher's Sourdough Rolls continue . . . . .
Dissolve yeast in warm water; mix with other ingredients. Set to rise in oiled or floured container until double in volume, about 1 - 2 hours. Punch down, roll into 1½" - 2" dough balls and place in bottom of a greased 14 inch Dutch oven. Allow to rise 1 hour. Brush top of rolls with melted butter or oil. Place 8 - 10 coals under the oven and place one ring of coals on top. Bake for 30 - 40 minutes. Cover the lid of the oven with coals for 2 - 3 minutes to brown the top of the rolls.

- Todd & Sissie Sandidge
Bandera, TX

Verona Lemon Bread

12 inch deep Dutch oven - Serves 10 - 12

2 pkgs. rapid rise yeast
1 cup warm water

- Add yeast to warm water and let stand for 10 minutes. After yeast is foamy add:
  6 Tbsp butter, softened

- In a large bowl thoroughly mix:
  1½ cups bread flour
  ½ cup sugar
  1 Tbsp grated lemon peel
  1½ tsp salt

- Gradually stir in yeast water to dry ingredients.
- Beat for 1 minute.
- Add:
  4 eggs, room temperature, beaten
  2 tsp vanilla
  ¼ cup bread flour

Beat vigorously for 2 minutes, stir in enough flour (about 4 cups) to make a soft dough.

Yeast Bread

- Cover, let rise in a warm place, free from drafts, until doubled in bulk, about 45 minutes.
- Turn dough out onto well floured board and knead for 1 minute and then roll dough to ½ inch thickness about 6" x 18" inches. Cut 3 Tbsp cold butter in small pieces and place on center 1/3 of dough. Fold 1/3 of dough over butter. Place another 3 Tbsp cold butter cut into small pieces on top of folded third of dough. Bring remaining 1/3 of dough over to cover butter and pinch edges closed.
- <u>Without adding more butter,</u> repeat rolling and folding procedure a total of 5 more times. Rolling dough out to a 6" x 18" inch long strip and folding into thirds.
- On a floured board, knead dough for 2 minutes and shape into a flat ball about the size of the oven bottom.
- Place in greased 12 inch deep Dutch oven. Cover and let rise in warm place, free from draft, until half doubled in bulk, about 35 to 50 minutes, depending on outside temperature.
- Bake at 350°F, **1 ring*** on bottom and **1½ rings*** on top for 40 minutes or until done. Add more charcoal to the lid at the end to brown the bread, if needed. Remove from oven and cool on wire rack.

Historical Note

This recipe came from the *Fleischmann's® Bake-it-Easy Yeast Book,* printed in 1972.

                                   - Dos Dinwiddies
                                 Duane & Sandy Dinwiddie
                                             Houston, TX

*See 'The Dinwiddie Method for Charcoal Briquet Use' on page 10.

Notes

Cakes

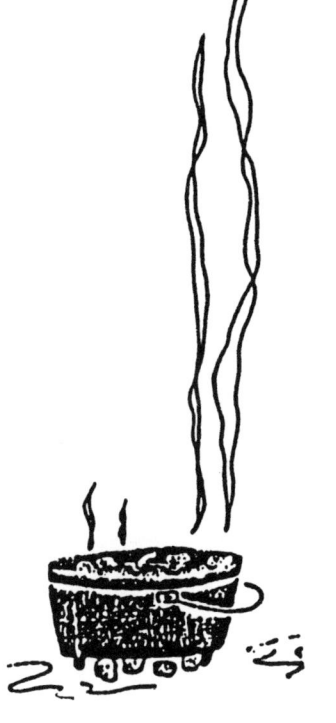

Apple Streusel Dutch Oven Cake
12 inch Dutch oven - Serves 16

Streusel:
1¼ cups packed light-brown sugar
¾ cup all-purpose flour
1 stick (½ cup) cold butter, cut into small pieces
2 tsp cinnamon
1 cup pecans, coarsely chopped

Cake:
3¼ cups all-purpose flour
1½ tsp baking powder
¾ tsp baking soda
1½ sticks (¾ cup) butter or margarine (not spread), softened
1¼ cups granulated sugar
3 large eggs
2 tsp vanilla
16 oz plain, low-fat, yogurt
2 apples, peeled, cored and cut into ½ inch pieces

Streusel: In a medium-size bowl, stir brown sugar, flour, butter and cinnamon with a fork or rub together with fingertips until crumbly and butter is completely incorporated. Stir in pecans.

Cake: Mix flour, baking powder and baking soda in a small bowl. Combine butter and sugar in a large bowl, stirring by hand. Add eggs, one at a time, beating well after each. Beat in vanilla and yogurt. Beat until fluffy. Beat in flour mixture just until blended, scraping down bowl as necessary.

Place 12 inch Dutch oven over 9 coals and preheat oven and lid. Oil the inside bottom of the oven with about 2 Tbsp of cooking oil. Spoon 3 cups of batter into pan and spread evenly. Sprinkle with ¼ cup of the streusel, the apples, then ½ cup of streusel. Spoon on remaining batter and spread evenly. Sprinkle with remaining streusel, pressing down lightly so it sticks to batter.

Place lid on Dutch oven. Checkerboard 17 coals on the lid. Bake 50 to 60 minutes or until a toothpick comes out clean. (You may need to add more coals mid-baking if they burn down too much to maintain cooking temperature.)

Remove lid and Dutch oven from fire to cool for about 15 minutes before serving.

- Mark & Pennie Prislovsky
Kerrville, TX

Apple Upside-Down Cake
14 inch Dutch oven

4 Tbsp butter
1 cup brown sugar, firmly packed
2 large baking apples
½ cup pecan halves
1 tsp cinnamon
1½ cups all-purpose flour
2 tsp baking powder
1/3 cup vegetable shortening
2/3 cup sugar
1 large egg
¾ tsp vanilla
¾ cup milk

Warm Dutch oven with 5 - 8 charcoal briquets and melt 4 Tbsp butter into oven. Take oven off coals and cool slightly. Sprinkle about 1/3 cup brown sugar into oven. Peel and core apples. Slice and lay over brown sugar. Sprinkle cinnamon over apples. Cover with balance of brown sugar and arrange pecan halves evenly.

In a large mixing bowl, sift flour and add baking powder and salt. Sift again. In another bowl, cream shortening with back of spoon. Add white sugar gradually. Cream together until light and fluffy. Add unbeaten egg and beat thoroughly. Add vanilla and milk to shortening and beat slightly.
Apple Upside-Down Cake continued. . . . . .

Apple Upside-Down Cake continued......

Add dry ingredients alternately with the liquid ingredients, stirring only enough after each addition to blend thoroughly. (It's important to alternate and not over beat.)

Pour batter over fruit and place oven over about 7 coals. Place 16 - 18 coals on lid and leave for 45 - 50 minutes.

Invert oven onto flat pan, using ample protection on hands and arms to prevent burning your skin. Let cake remain in inverted oven for a minute or two to allow syrup to drain onto cake.

Serve with whipped cream.

- William & Marilyn D'Lizarraga
Sulphur Springs, TX

Apple Pecan Crumb Cake

12 inch Dutch oven

CAKE:
3 cups flour
1½ Tbsp baking powder
½ tsp salt
¼ cup butter or margarine
1½ cups sugar
3 eggs
¾ cup + 1½ Tbsp milk
2 tsp vanilla
1 - 20 oz can apple pie filling

STRUESEL:
1¼ cups light-brown sugar, packed
¼ cup flour
½ cup cold butter or margarine, diced
2 tsp cinnamon
1 cup pecans, chopped

Grease a 12 inch Dutch oven.

STREUSEL: In medium bowl, stir brown sugar, flour, butter and cinnamon until crumbly and butter is thoroughly mixed in. Stir in pecans.

CAKE: Combine flour, baking powder and salt. Set aside. Cream butter, add sugar and beat until fluffy. Add eggs and mix well. Stir in flour mixture alternately with milk beginning and ending with milk. Add vanilla and beat well.

Pour half of cake mixture in oven. Sprinkle ¼ th of the streusel over the batter then add the apples, and ½ of the streusel. Spoon the remaining batter carefully on top and sprinkle with remaining ¼ th streusel. Cover and place over 10 briquets. Place 14 briquets on top. Rotate lid counter-clock wise ¼ of a turn and oven clockwise ¼ of a turn every ten minutes. After 30 - 40 minutes take all heat off the bottom and continue baking for another 20 minutes, rotating lid counter-clockwise 1/4 of a turn every ten minutes.

- Scott & Debbie Ragland
Duncanville, TX]

Banana Coconut Cake

2 - 10 inch Dutch ovens

1½ cups shortening
3 cups sugar
4 eggs
2 cups mashed ripe bananas
2 tsp vanilla extract
4 cups cake flour
2 tsp baking soda
2 tsp baking powder
1 tsp salt
1 cup buttermilk
2 cups coconut flakes

BUTTER CREAM FROSTING:
1 cup shortening
1 cup margarine, softened
4 cups confectioner's sugar
1 tsp vanilla
1 tsp coconut extract
pinch of salt
½ cup evaporated milk

Banana Coconut Cake continued. . . . .

Lone Star Dutch Oven Society Cookbook

Banana Coconut Cake continued. . . . .
In a mixing bowl, cream shortening and sugar until fluffy. Add eggs: beat by hand for two minutes. Add bananas and vanilla; beat for two minutes. Combine dry ingredients, add to creamed mixture alternately with buttermilk. Mix well. Pour into two well greased and floured 10 inch Dutch ovens, in even amounts. Sprinkle each with coconut. Bake at 375°F (approximately 6 coals on the bottom and 10 coals on top for each oven) for 25 - 30 minutes or until cakes tests done. Loosely cover with foil during last 10 minutes of baking. Cool in ovens away from fire for about 10 minutes, then place on inverted Dutch oven lids, one coconut side up and one coconut side down.

Frosting: In a mixing bowl, cream shortening and margarine. Add remaining frosting ingredients. Mix by hand until well blended and smooth, keep mixing until all lumps from sugar have disappeared. Spread frosting evenly on top of cake with coconut side down. Next top with second layer, coconut side up; frost sides and 1 inch around top edge of cake, leaving coconut center showing.

Historical Note

This recipe come from the **T4- Ranch**, located between Medina and Bandera, TX. This cake was often baked at the close of shearing season. The same shearing crew usually went from ranch to ranch in the Bandera County area and were treated to many mouth watering meals.

- by the cooking team of
Bill Spangler & Ike Craddock
Medina, TX

Cakes

Bunted Pumpkin Cake

Deep 14 inch Dutch oven - Feeds 12 - 16 people

1¼ cups sugar	2½ cups flour
½ cup cooking oil	3 Tbsp baking powder
3 eggs	1 tsp cinnamon
1 cup pumpkin	½ tsp ginger
¾ cup milk	½ tsp nutmeg
½ tsp baking soda	½ tsp salt

Grease bundt pan with shortening, dust with flour and preheat your Dutch oven to 325°F. Mix until creamy in a medium-size bowl the sugar and cooking oil. Then blend in the eggs, pumpkin, milk and baking soda. Add the remaining ingredients and continue mixing for 4 to 6 minutes. After mixing fold in ¾ cup of chopped pecans. Pour into bundt pan. Place the bundt pan on a trivet or rack in the Dutch oven. Bake until springy to touch. Remove from oven. Let stand for 5 minutes. Dump out on a rack to cool. Drizzle icing on top.

Thin Brown Sugar Icing:

¼ cup brown sugar	2 Tbsp heavy cream
2 Tbsp butter	dash of salt
1½ cups powdered sugar	

Combine all ingredients except powdered sugar and heat in a metal bowl or very small Dutch oven just until brown sugar dissolves. Remove from heat. Blend in 1½ cups of powdered sugar. When smooth, pour over cake while both are slightly warm.

Historical Note

This recipe was copied from Joan Larsen' *Lovin' Dutch Ovens* cookbook. I have cooked it several times for different groups and it always worked well - it also always brought pleasant smiles to everyone's faces.

                                    - Hatfield Ranch Cocineros
                                    Dan Hatfield & Cindy Rather
                                            Medina, TX

Carrot Cake

14 inch Dutch oven - Serves 12 - 16

Cake:
Combine the following ingredients:

2 cups unsifted flour	2 tsp cinnamon
2 cups sugar	1 tsp salt
2 tsp soda	1 cup oil

Next add:
4 eggs, one at a time beating well after each

Then add:
3 cups peeled, grated carrots and mix thoroughly

Pour prepared cake batter into a greased and lightly floured 14 inch Dutch oven. Cook with **1 ring*** of charcoal on the bottom and **1½ rings*** on top (350°F) for about 35 minutes. Cake is done when a toothpick inserted into center comes out clean and cake is gently pulling away from edges of the oven. Cool cake for at least 30 minutes before frosting.

Frosting ingredients:
1 - 8 oz pkg. cream cheese, softened
1 stick (½ cup) butter, softened
4 cups powdered sugar
1 tsp vanilla
½ cup chopped pecans, (to sprinkle on top of frosting for decoration- optional)

Beat cream cheese and butter together until smooth an fluffy. Add powdered sugar 1/3 at a time, mixing well after each addition. Mix in vanilla.

Historical Note

This cake is a popular one all over the country. We were first introduced to it in Madison, Wisconsin, in 1973

- Dos Dinwiddies
Duane & Sandy Dinwiddie
Houston, TX

Dutch Oven Friendship Cake

Choose a gallon jar with a spouted lid or cover with a dish cloth

Pour into a gallon jar: 1½ cups starter juice (or brandy)
2½ cups sugar
1 - 29 oz can sliced peaches & juice

*Stir every day and
on the 10th day add:*   1 - 20 oz can chunk pineapple & juice
2½ cups sugar

*Stir every day and
on the 20th day add:*   2 - 9 oz jars chopped maraschino cherries & juice
2½ cups sugar

*Stir every day and
<u>on the 30th day drain off the fruit and reserve the starter juice</u>*

Preheat oven by making a ring of coals a little bigger than the bottom of the Dutch oven. Place approximately 10 coals on the lid. After heating the oven, grease with shortening.

Combine   2 cups sugar
1½ cups oil or butter
4 eggs
¼ cup water

Add dry ingredients: 2 cups flour
1 small box instant pudding mix (any flavor)
½ tsp salt
2 tsp baking soda

Mix together well
and add: 1¼ cup of drained fruit
1 cup chopped walnuts

Bake in Dutch oven for 30 - 45 minutes. Cake is done when a knife stuck into the center comes out clean. Cake should be a rich golden brown.

Dutch Oven Friendship Cake continued. . . . .

Dutch Oven Friendship Cake continued. . . . .

There will be enough fruit to make 3 cakes and enough starter juice for 3 friends (thus the name 'Friendship Cake') and one for yourself to begin again. The juice never goes bad if kept at room temperature in a jar with a loose lid. I have had my starter for 15 years. Don't be tempted to substitute the starter juice for water in the recipe. It will not cook up properly.

- The Cherokee Chef
Bonita Sanders
Seabrook, TX

German Festive Cake

12 inch Dutch oven - 12 to 16 servings

1 pkg. Duncan Hines® Deluxe Swiss Chocolate Cake Mix
1 cup almonds, chopped   3 eggs
1 tsp cinnamon   ½ cup oil
1 tsp almond extract   2 cups firm ripe bananas,
1 - 8 oz can drained crushed pineapple   chopped

Preheat 12 inch Dutch oven to 350°F (10 coals on bottom and 14 coals on top). Grease a 10 inch tube pan.

Combine dry cake mix, almonds and cinnamon in a large bowl. Beat eggs slightly; stir in oil, almond extract, bananas, and pineapple. Add to dry ingredients and mix thoroughly with spoon; do not beat. Turn batter into pan and spread evenly.

Place a rack or trivet inside Dutch oven and place tube pan on top of rack. Bake using **1 ring*** of coals on the bottom and **1½ rings*** of coals on the top for 45 - 55 minutes; cake is done when toothpick inserted in center comes out clean. Sprinkle cooled cake with powdered sugar.

- Mc Carthy & Sainlar

*See 'The Dinwiddie Method of Charcoal Briquet Use' on page 10.

Grandmother Cora's Chocolate Pan Cake
14 inch Dutch oven - Serves 10 - 12

Sift together:
> 2 cups sugar
> 2 cups flour

Bring the following ingredients to a rapid boil, pour over flour & sugar and stir:
> 1 stick (½ cup) butter
> ½ cup Crisco® shortening
> 4 Tbsp cocoa
> 1 cup water

Add to above mixture and stir until well blended:
> ½ cup buttermilk
> 2 eggs, lightly beaten
> 1 tsp baking soda
> 1 tsp cinnamon
> 1 tsp vanilla

Grease and flour a 14 inch Dutch oven. Pour cake batter into oven. (Make sure that oven is level). Place **2 rings*** of charcoal on top and **1 ring*** underneath. Bake for 20 to 25 minutes or until cake is done. Cake is done when toothpick inserted into cake comes out clean. Cool cake for approximately 15 to 20 minutes in the oven.

Icing:
In an 8 inch Dutch oven, melt together and bring to boil, stirring constantly, the following ingredients:
> 1 stick (½ cup butter)
> 4 Tbsp cocoa
> 6 Tbsp milk

Then add the hot liquid to the following ingredients and beat with a spoon until creamy:
> 4 cups sifted powdered sugar
> 1 tsp vanilla

Grandmother Cora's Chocolate Pan Cake continued. . . . .

Grandmother Cora's Chocolate Pan Cake continued.....
Pour over cake immediately. Decorate with chopped pecans or with White Bark curls. When cool the icing will be like fudge.

Historical Note
This chocolate pan cake is a family favorite, handed down from my grandmother Cora Hayes of Birmingham, Alabama. The exact age of the recipe is unknown, but it is at least 100 years old.

- Dos Dinwiddies
Duane & Sandy Dinwiddie
Houston, TX

*See 'The Dinwiddie Method of Charcoal Briquet Use' on page 10.

Honey-Glazed Apple Pecan Cake
12 inch or 14 inch Dutch oven - Serves 8 - 10

Note: you will need an extra Dutch oven, spider or skillet and 12 extra lighted coals to prepare parts of this recipe.

Glaze:
½ cup honey
½ cup sugar
¼ cup water
2 Tbsp lemon juice
1 cinnamon stick

Cake:
2½ to 3 cups green apples, peeled cored and cut into 1 inch cubes or slices
1 cup butter, softened
1½ cups sugar
1½ tsp vanilla
5 eggs
2 cups flour
1 Tbsp baking powder
1 Tbsp cinnamon
¾ cup pecans, chopped

Cakes

- Light your coals first so they will be hot when the cake is all mixed. <u>Check the coals before doing step 5.</u> If necessary, delay step 5 until the coals are ready to use.
- Using the extra skillet or Dutch oven and coals, lightly sauté apple chunks in 2 Tbsp butter. Set aside.
- In a bowl, cream remaining butter with sugar until light and fluffy. Beat in vanilla. Beat in eggs one at a time.
- In a bowl, sift together flour, baking powder and cinnamon.
- **Step 5** - Stir into butter mixture until blended. Fold in apples and pecans.
- Spoon into well-seasoned Dutch oven. You can grease and flour the oven if you have trouble with things sticking.
- Use the amount of coals appropriate for the size oven you are using.
- Bake at 350°F (see temperature controls on pages 11 & 12):
    12 inch Dutch oven - 1 hour
    14 inch Dutch oven - 45 minutes to 1 hour
        (the cake will be slightly thinner)
- Cake is done when a toothpick inserted near the center will come out clean.
- While the cake is baking make the glaze.
- In a skillet or Dutch oven, heat the honey, sugar, water, lemon juice, and cinnamon stick. Let this simmer for 10 minutes, remove from heat but keep warm until the cake is done. Add water sparingly if the glaze starts to thicken.
- When cake is done let it cool about 15 minutes. Remove cinnamon stick from glaze, then, with a pastry brush, paint the warm cake with glaze. Repeat until all the glaze is used up

This cake can be served hot, warm or cold - excellent with a scoop of ice cream on top. The cake can be frozen if you want to save some. To defrost, place cake in refrigerator the day you plan to serve it.

Historical Note

This was modified from a recipe said to be by Edie Greenberg, food editor of the San Diego Jewish Times.

- Mike & Ed Galucki
Cabot, AR

Larapin Pineapple Upside-Down Cake
12 inch Dutch Oven

¼ lb (1 stick = ½ cup) butter or margarine
¾ bag brown sugar
1 can pineapple, sliced
1 can crushed pineapple
1 small jar maraschino cherries, drained
½ cup shortening, melted
1½ cups sugar
1 tsp vanilla
2 eggs, slightly beaten
2 cups flour
2½ tsp baking powder
1 tsp salt
1 cup milk

In a 12 inch Dutch oven, melt ¼ lb butter, add brown sugar and let it absorb the butter.

Place pineapple slices over brown sugar mixture and place a cherry in each pineapple hole. Sprinkle the crushed pineapple over this.

In a separate pan, mix the flour, baking powder, sugar, and salt. Add melted shortening, vanilla, slightly beaten eggs, and milk to flour mixture. Mix well and pour over pineapple.

Place Dutch oven over 8 charcoal briquets and cover the lid with charcoal. Cook for about 45 minutes

Cake should be brown on top. Insert a knife or stick in the cake, if it comes out clean, the cake is done. Turn the Dutch oven over (be careful, it is hot) on a large pan or piece of foil. Enjoy!

- Chloice & Vance Shofner
Midland, TX

Mr. Austin's Delight

12 inch Dutch oven - Serves 14 - 16

3½ cups flour
3 apples, pared, cored, and chopped
1 cup corn oil
2 tsp vanilla
3 eggs
2 cups brown sugar
1 cup pecans, chopped
2 Tbsp saleratus (baking powder is the modern equivalent)
1 Tbsp cinnamon
1 Tbsp cloves

Blend all ingredients together.

Pre-heat the Dutch oven for 15 minutes with 15 briquets on the lid and 12 underneath. Pour the batter into the pre-heated oven. Bake at 400°F for 20 minutes with 16 briquets on the lid and 8 underneath. Bake an additional 30 minutes with 24 briquets on the lid and 8 underneath.

Historical Note

Wheat and apples do not grow well in Austin's colony. Mr. Samuel May Williams, secretary to Mr. Stephen F. Austin, procured a barrel of both apples and wheat flour on his last trip to Galveston from a ship's captain bound to Veracrus from Philadelphia. His intent was to prepare a favorite apple cake he remembered from his childhood in the eastern United States. The recipe published here is his second attempt. He left out the saleratus in his first cake which produced a soggy glop. When Mr. Austin, accustomed to the corn meal confections of the colony, first tasted this cake he is reported to have exclaimed, "Mr. Williams, your cake is a delight!"

- Los Cocineros de Arroyo Seco
Carl S. Hacker & Claudia A Kozinetz
Houston, TX

Oatmeal Cake

14 inch Dutch oven - Serves 12

1¼ cup boiling water
1 cup oatmeal
½ cup sugar
1 cup light brown sugar, packed
1 tsp vanilla

2 eggs
1½ cups flour
1 tsp baking soda
¾ tsp cinnamon
½ tsp nutmeg

Bring water to a boil and pour over oatmeal, let stand for 20 minutes. Beat butter, add sugar, brown sugar, vanilla and eggs. When mixed well stir in oatmeal. Sift flour, baking soda, salt, cinnamon, and nutmeg in a separate bowl. Add flour mixture to butter mixture. Grease and flour a 14 inch Dutch oven. Pour in mixture. Place Dutch oven over 10 - 15 coals and place 15 - 20 coals on the lid. Bake for 25 - 30 minutes, then remove from bottom coals. Bake with coals on the top for 10 - 15 minutes or until it is done.

Frosting:
¼ cup butter, melted
½ cup brown sugar, packed
3 Tbsp evaporated milk

Bring all ingredients to a boil for 3 minutes then chill.

Let cake cool for 15 to 20 minutes before pouring frosting over the cake.

- Todd & Sissie Sandidge
Bandera, TX

Cakes

Orange Pound Cake

12 inch Dutch oven - Feeds 10 - 14 adults or 2 - 3 teenagers

Cake:
1 cup butter or margarine, softened
½ cup shortening
3 cups sugar
5 large eggs
3 cups all-purpose flour
1 tsp salt
½ tsp baking powder
1 cup milk
1 Tbsp orange extract
1 Tbsp orange peel, grated
1 Tbsp orange food coloring

Glaze:
1 to 1¼ cups powdered sugar
¼ cup butter or margarine, softened
2 Tbsp orange juice
1 tsp grated orange peel

In a large mixing bowl, cream butter, shortening, and sugar until light & fluffy. Add eggs, one at a time, beating well after each addition.

Combine flour, salt, and baking powder. Gradually add dry ingredients to creamed mix, alternately, with the milk. Mix well after each addition. Add orange extract, peel, and food coloring, mixing well.

Pour into greased and lightly floured oven, use 8 briquets under and 17 on lid, bake at 350°F for about 1¼ hours or until done. Test doneness with a straw. May need to add new hot briquets, 3 under and 5 on lid, to finish baking.

If using glaze, combine all ingredients and drizzle over cooled cake. We decorated this cake by placing canned mandarin orange slices on top instead of using glaze, however, both may be used. For kitchen ovens, pour batter into a greased fluted tube cake pan; bake at 350°F for about 70 minutes or until cake tests done. Turn out onto a rack to cool and then glaze or decorate as desired.

Historical Note
We have modified this recipe from a lemon pound cake recipe in *The BEST of Country Cooking,* Second Edition, available from
Orange Pound Cake continued. . . . .

Orange Pound Cake continued. . . . .
Reiman Publications, L.P. 5400 S. 60 Street, Greendale, WI 53129. This is an excellent cake for kids (and adults) at parties or special occasion (or anytime)!

- The Two B's Dutch Oven Team
Bill & Beverly Brummel
San Antonio, TX

Peppermint Pound Cake
12 inch Dutch oven - will feed 8 - 10 adults or 2 teenagers

1 cup vegetable shortening
2 cups sugar
4 eggs
3 tsp peppermint extract
1 tsp butter flavoring
½ tsp salt
3 cups flour
¾ cup buttermilk
½ cup peppermint candy, crushed

Cream shortening and sugar. Add eggs and beat well. Mix in extract, flavoring and salt. Add flour and butter in small amounts, stirring well. When batter is thoroughly mixed, add crushed candy and stir throughout gently. Pour batter into greased and floured oven, use 8 briquets under and 17 on oven's lid. Bake at 350°F for about 1 hour or until done. Test if done with a piece of straw or a toothpick.

Glaze for cake:
Blend one cup of powdered sugar with 2 Tbsp sweet milk and ¼ tsp peppermint extract. Drizzle over top of cake. Serve and enjoy!

Historical Note
We've adapted this recipe from one found in *Dutch Oven Cooking* by John G. Ragsdale. Copies of this book are available though the Boy Scouts of America. This recipe may be used in a bundt cake pan in your home oven. Keeping any of this cake for serving the next day will be very difficult if not impossible! Kids from 2 to 92 years old absolutely love it and will quickly snitch a piece when the cake is left unguarded!

- The Two B's Dutch Oven Team
Bill & Beverly Brummel
San Antonio, TX

Pioneer Journey Cake

12 inch Dutch oven - Serves 8 - 10

Cream until light:
    1½ cups sugar
    ¼ cup butter

Mix in : 2½ cups apple cider

Add: 1 tsp baking soda
         1 tsp cinnamon
         1 tsp cloves
         ½ cup dried apples, chopped fine

Blend in: 4½ cups flour

Beat until batter is well mixed, then pour into prepared Dutch oven and bake at 375°F. Set up oven with 18 charcoal briquets on top and 11 underneath. Bake for 25 - 30 minutes or until straw inserted in center comes out clean. Remove from heat and let cool 15 - 20 minutes. Serve directly from oven. Serve with fresh churned butter and old-fashioned molasses.

Historical Note

This recipe was made by the early western settlers. It called for the basics carried in every wagon, but not fresh milk or eggs, which were harder to come by. Although heavier textured that today's cakes, it still has a great flavor. For variety, sprinkle cinnamon and sugar on top before baking. Also try a variety of dried fruits like dried apricots, cherries, or currents. Chopped pecans might also be added.

Pioneer Journey Cake continued. . . . .

Pioneer Journey Cake continued......
This recipe was found in *Lovin' Dutch Ovens* by Joan S. Larsen. Published by LFS Publications, Salt Lake City, UT 84119

> - The Oven Lovin' Team
> Judy & Jamie Ragland
> Duncanville, TX

Strawberry Swirl Coffee Cake

12 inch Dutch oven - Makes 16 servings

¼ cup plus 1 tsp sugar
¼ cup warm water
1 - ¼ oz pkg. active dry yeast
1 egg
¼ cup vegetable oil
1 cup milk

3 to 4 cups all-purpose flour
½ cup chopped pecans
2/3 cup finely crushed crisp coconut cookies
4 Tbsp butter, melted
1 cup strawberry jam or preserves

Combine the 1 tsp sugar, warm water, and yeast in a small bowl. Stir to mix. Set aside until bubbly.

In a large bowl, combine the remaining ¼ cup sugar, egg, oil, milk, and salt. Stir to mix. Add 1 cup of the flour and mix. Stir in the yeast mixture. Add enough of the remaining flour to make a soft dough. Knead the dough on a lightly floured surface until smooth. Place in an oiled bowl. Turn so that all the dough is coated with the oil. Cover and let rise in a warm place until light and doubled in bulk. This should take about 1 hour.

While the dough is rising, prepare the nut filling. In a small bowl, combine the chopped pecans and the crushed cookies.

After the dough has risen, punch it down and divide it into 3 equal pieces. On a lightly floured surface, roll one portion of the dough into a 12 inch circle. Don't worry if the circle is not exact because this dough can be pulled to correct size. Place the first circle into the

Dutch oven. Brush with 2 Tbsp of the melted butter. Sprinkle with half the cookie mixture. Continue with the next portion of dough. After it is rolled, place it on top of the first circle. Spread the jam over the dough. Roll the third portion into a 12 inch circle and place on top of the jam-covered circle. Brush with remaining 2 Tbsp of butter and sprinkle with remaining cookie mixture.

Place a glass (about 2 inches in diameter) upside down in the center of the circle. Do not press it into the dough. The glass is used only to mark the center. Cut the dough into 16 wedges, cutting just to the glass. Twist each three-layered section five times, and lay back in the Dutch oven. Remove the glass. Cover and allow to rise until doubled. This should take 40 - 45 minutes.

Bake at 375°F (**1 ring*** on the bottom and **1½ rings*** on top) and for 20 - 25 minutes, until golden brown and no longer doughy. Cool slightly.

Glaze:
To make the glaze, combine 1½ cups powdered sugar, 2 - 3 Tbsp milk, and ¼ tsp vanilla extract into a small bowl. Drizzle over coffee cake.

Historical Note
I found this recipe in *A Treasury of Southern Baking* cookbook. It is not as hard to make as it sounds and always comes out tasting great.

- Hatfield Ranch Cocineros
Dan Hatfield & Cindy Rather
Medina, TX

*See 'The Dinwiddie Method of Charcoal Briquet Use' on page 10.

Texas Dutch Oven Pecan Cake

12 inch Dutch oven - Makes a large cake

Mix together in a small bowl and let stand for 30 minutes. Stir occasionally:

    1 - 15 oz box golden raisins
    1 cup bourbon whiskey

2 cups + 2 Tbsp butter, softened
2¼ cups sugar
2¼ tsp baking powder
4½ cups flour
4½ cups pecans, coarsely chopped
8 eggs

1½ tsp salt
1½ cups bourbon whiskey
2¼ tsp ground nutmeg

Generously butter Dutch oven and flour lightly. Set aside. Cream butter and sugar until light and fluffy. Beat in eggs one at a time.

In another bowl, mix together flour, baking powder, nutmeg, salt and chopped pecans. Add this, one cup full at a time, to creamed mixture mixing well after each addition.

With a slotted spoon transfer raisins to cake batter. Using the bourbon the raisins have not soaked in, add more bourbon to measure 1½ cups and add to cake batter. Mix well.

Pour batter into butter and floured Dutch oven. Bake for about 50 - 60 minutes or until cake tests done. Use **1 ring*** of charcoal briquets on the bottom and **1½ rings*** on the top. Let cake cool in oven about 20 - 30 minutes then turn out on lid. Drizzle with Praline Glaze.

Praline Glaze

½ cup brown sugar, firmly packed
¼ cup white sugar
¼ cup butter
¼ whipping cream
½ cup pecan halves

Combine first four ingredients in a Dutch oven. Cook over low heat (**half a ring*** of coals) stirring constantly, until mixture reaches soft ball stage. Remove from heat and stir in pecans. Drizzle over warm cake.

- Shem Ray & Noah Ray
Sulphur Springs, TX

*See 'The Dinwiddie Method of Charcoal Briquet Use' on page 10.

Thank You, Johnny

12 inch Dutch oven - Serves 14 - 16

6 cups apples (Granny Smith type), peeled & diced
1½ cups sugar
4 eggs, well beaten
4 cups flour, sifted
6 tsp cinnamon
4 tsp baking soda
2 cups chopped pecans

Mix sugar with apples and let stand until sugar is dissolved. Add well beaten eggs, stir in well. Sift dry ingredients together and stir into apple mixture, add pecans, pour into an oiled 12 inch Dutch oven. Bake at 375°F for 40 minutes or until top is browned and springs back when pressed. Use 10 briquets underneath the oven and 18 - 20 briquets on top of lid. Remove oven from heat when done and immediately pour hot glaze over the top of crust. <u>Wait 'til you taste this - but let it cool some or you'll burn your tongue!</u>

HOT GLAZE
1 cup brown sugar	1 cup sugar
4 Tbsp flour	2 cups water
½ cup butter/margarine	2 tsp vanilla
¼ tsp salt	

Thank You, Johnny continued. . . . .

Thank You, Johnny continued. . . . .
Heat all to boiling stage in sauce pan. Lower heat to simmer and simmer slowly for 10 minutes, stirring frequently to prevent burning. Pour over top of 'Thank You, Johnny' cake.

Historical Note

Johnny Appleseed was always thanked profusely for scattering all those apple seeds wherever he went. The apples from these trees made life more enjoyable for the early pioneer people, for cooking, just plain eatin', cider, vinegar and that all important applejack.

- Larry & Bungy Hartshorn
Bandera, TX

Notes

Desserts

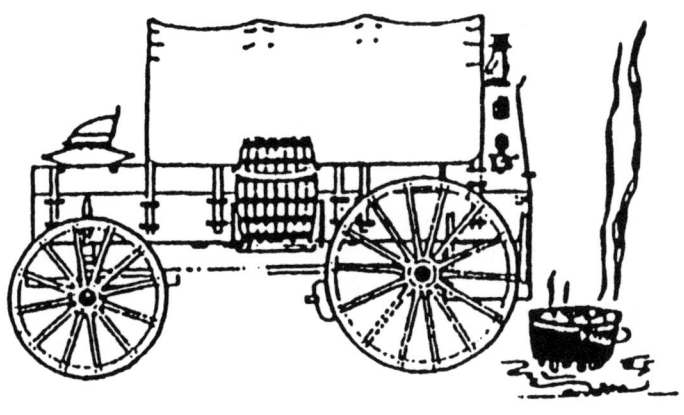

Passel O' Pumpkin
12 inch Dutch oven

2 - 15 oz cans solid pack pumpkin
3 carrots, medium, fine grated
4 eggs, slightly beaten
1½ cups sugar
1 cup raisins
½ cup shredded coconut
1 tsp salt
½ tsp mace
½ tsp cinnamon
1 tsp ginger, ground
½ tsp cloves, ground
4 drops oil of anise
3 cups evaporated milk (2 cans of Carnation®)

TOPPING:
1 pkg. yellow cake mix
½ cup butter (1 stick)
1 cup pecans, chopped
12 pecan halves, whole for garnish
12 maraschino cherries, sliced

Mix together in a large bowl, pumpkin, shredded carrots, eggs, sugar, raisins coconut, salt, mace, cinnamon, ginger, cloves, anise and milk. Pour into slightly oiled and heated 12 inch Dutch oven.

TOPPING: Sprinkle dry cake mix, evenly, over pumpkin mixture in oven, drizzle melted butter over topping and scatter chopped pecans over topping. Bake at 425°F for 20 minutes, then reduce heat to 350°F for 50 minutes or until knife/toothpick comes out clean. Make sure oven and contents are at 425°F for the full 20 minutes time - use 20 new coals on top and 12 under. For 350°F use 14 good coals on top and 6 underneath oven. Be careful not a overheat bottom of the pudding. Also, keep watch of topping to achieve a rich golden brown color.

GARNISH: After baking, neatly space whole pecan halves over surface. Slice cherries, vertically, into 1/8 ths, and form rosettes around pecan halves.

Historical Note

This recipe was inspired by a Mexican filled pan dulce (pastry), which was served at the EL TACO VAQUERO Restaurant in Bandera, TX and on both sides of the Rio Grande.

- Larry & Bungy Hartshorn
Bandera, TX

Apple-Pecan Dutch Oven Ice Cream?

12 inch Dutch oven - Serves 8

12 lb. ice
1 box Morton® salt

ICE CREAM MIX:
- 2 cups milk
- 1 small pkg. instant vanilla pudding
- ½ cup sugar
- 1 egg
- ½ Tbsp vanilla
- ¼ tsp fresh lemon juice
- 1 cup whipping cream
- 1 - 12 oz can evaporated milk

TOPPING:
- ½ cup pecans, finely chopped
- ½ cup Granny Smith apples, finely chopped
- ½ cup dried apples, finely chopped
- ¼ cup brown sugar
- ¼ tsp cinnamon
- 3 Tbsp butter

Fix topping first:
Preheat Dutch oven with 16 briquets under the bottom. Melt 3 Tbsp butter. Add apples (both fresh and dried) and fry apples for about 3 minutes, or until dried apples start to brown. Add pecans
Apple-Pecan Dutch Oven Ice Cream? continued. . . . .

Apple-Pecan Dutch Oven Ice Cream? continued. . . . .
and cook for 1 more minute. Remove from butter, drain and place in a bowl with brown sugar and cinnamon, mix well. Set aside to cool. (This may be cooked in a skillet on the side.)
Wash and cool down the Dutch oven!!! (A hot oven will crack and shatter if cooled too fast.)

Ice Cream:
Mix instant pudding with 2 cups milk. In a separate bowl, mix ½ cup sugar, 1 egg, ½ Tbsp vanilla, and ¼ tsp lemon juice. Add to pudding mixture. Pour mixture into a dry and cool 12 inch Dutch oven. Place oven in a 16 inch bowl. Arrange crushed ice and rock salt around oven as you would in an ice cream freezer (layers of 1 inch ice and 1/4 to 1/2 inch of salt) Placing ice on the lid will cool the oven down faster, (no salt and no deeper than the lip). Lift the lid and stir every 2 to 5 minutes. It will go slow at first until the oven cools down. Add ice and salt to the bowl as needed.

The *Topping* may be mixed into the ice cream before it sets up hard or used as a topping.

The ice cream may be eaten soft, or if you prefer harder ice cream you may place ice and rock salt on the lid. (Don't spill the water into the Dutch oven.)

Total freezing time is 30 - 45 minutes.

- The Chuckle Wagon Cookers
Steve & Jeanice Bias
La Marque, TX

Aunt Hetty's Bread Pudding
12 inch Dutch oven

1 cup sugar	1 Tbsp vanilla extract
1 stick (½ cup) butter	¼ cup golden raisins
5 eggs, beaten	12 slices day old French bread
1 pint (2 cups) half & half cream	1 tsp cinnamon
Rum Sauce (recipe follows)	

- Cream together sugar and butter in a large bowl. Gradually add half & half cream and then add beaten eggs, cinnamon, vanilla, raisins, and mix well.
- In order to bake this pudding, it must be placed in a Pyrex® or Corning Ware® dish inside a 12 inch Dutch oven. It must be place on a small trivet so that the dish holding the pudding is not in direct contact with the bottom of the Dutch oven. We use a 8½" x 3" deep Pyrex® bowl.
- Cut the bread into approximately 1 inch squares and place these in the bowl to soak in the pudding mixture. Use a spatula to push the cubes to the bottom of the mix. This will help expel air and saturate the bread. Let the bread cubes soak for at least 30 minutes.
- Preheat a 12 inch Dutch oven to 350°F, by using 17 briquets on the lid and about 7 briquets underneath. Cover the bowl with a piece of aluminum foil and place the bowl in the Dutch oven on the trivet. Bake for about 1 hour 10 minutes. When the pudding is almost "set", remove the foil and allow the pudding to brown on top, for an additional 10 - 15 minutes.

RUM SAUCE

1 cup butter	½ cup half & half cream
½ cup sugar	2 Tbsp dark rum

Combine butter, sugar & cream in a heavy saucepan; cook over a medium heat until the sugar dissolves. Bring to a boil, reduce heat & simmer 5 minutes. Let cook and then add rum or rum flavoring. Serve this sauce over the pudding.

- Los Dos Compadres
  Wayne Adam & Gary Grogan
  Wharton, TX

Bodacious Baked Pears
12 inch Dutch oven - 6 large or 12 small servings

6 firm but ripe Bartlett pears
4 - 6 Tbsp light brown sugar
2 - 3 Tbsp cinnamon
4 - 6 crumbled butter cookies
½ cup pecan pieces
6 - 12 pecan halves
pinch of ground cloves for each pear half
butter

Preheat the 12 inch Dutch oven with a light coating of butter on the inside bottom, using 8 to 10 briquets underneath. Peel and halve the pears. With a small spoon or melon baller, scoop out the seeds. Sprinkle lightly with ground cloves. Stuff the pears with a mixture of crumbled butter cookies, brown sugar, cinnamon and pecan pieces. Put the pear halves in the oven, cut sides up. Dot with butter and then with 1 to 2 pecan halves for each pear half. Cover and add 12 - 14 briquets to the top of oven. Cook until hot, about 20 - 30 minutes. Serve immediately. Ice cream is great with this.

- Shuler Land and Livestock Company
Brian & Mat Shuler
Wylie, TX

Chocolate M-M-M-M-M-M.
12 inch Dutch oven - Serves 8 - 10

¾ cup raisins, brown or golden
1½ cups warm water
1½ cups light brown sugar, firmly packed
½ cup sugar
¾ cup unsweetened cocoa
9 large eggs, lightly beaten
7½ cups milk

Desserts

3 Tbsp butter or margarine
2 tsp vanilla extract
1 tsp almond extract
½ tsp salt
2 tsp nutmeg
¾ cup walnuts, chopped
12 cups white bread, cut into 1/2" cubes (about 24 slices)
12 maraschino cherries, sliced into quarters

- Soak raisins in warm water in a small bowl, let stand for 10 - 15 minutes until softened. Drain raisins, discard water, set aside.
- Whisk the light brown sugar and white sugar with the cocoa and eggs in a bowl until smooth. Set aside. Heat milk and butter in a sauce pan over low heat until the butter melts - about 3 minutes. Whisk milk mixture into cocoa mixture along with vanilla, almond, salt, nutmeg, ½ cup of raisins, ½ cup chopped nuts.
- Place the bread cubes in a lightly oiled 12 inch Dutch oven. Sprinkle with the balance of the raisins, then pour in the cocoa mixture. Sprinkle remaining chopped walnuts over the top, evenly. Let stand for 10 minutes.
- Cover the Dutch oven and cook at 375°F - 400°F for 15 minutes (17 coals on top and 12 coals underneath). Then lower heat to 350°F - 375°F for 10 minutes or until a toothpick inserted in the center comes out clean. (14 coals on top and 9 coals underneath.)
- Garnish with cherry slices. Serve warm not hot, or at room temperature for best taste experience.

Historical Note

Out on the trail, an ol' chuck wagon 'coosie' I used to know, made up a puddin' with left over biscuits that would be mostly dried or stale. Mixed with canned milk, eggs - if the cowpokes could find a turkey clutch - a little flour, vanilla, sugar, dried raisins and whatever. He said, "They horsed it down 's if it woz their last meal." In time, Mr. Hershey's cocoa found it's way out on to the range and into the pudding. "It then became a must, or those cowpokes would make up some miserable trick to pull on me, like hiding a cactus in my bed-roll."

- Larry & Bungy Hartshorn
Bandera, TX

Explorador Bread Pudding

3 large eggs
1¼ cups sugar
1½ tsp vanilla extract
1¼ tsp ground nutmeg
1¼ tsp ground cinnamon

¼ cup butter, melted
2 cups milk
½ cup raisins
½ cup pecans, coarsely chopped
5 cups French bread cubes

SAUCE:
8 oz (1 cup) butter
2 cups powdered sugar

2 large eggs
1 oz rum extract

In a bowl, beat eggs with metal whisk (for about 6 minutes). Add sugar, vanilla, nutmeg, cinnamon & butter. Beat until well blended. Beat in the milk, then stir in raisins and pecans.

Place the bread cubes in a greased Dutch oven. Pour the egg mixture over the cubes and toss until bread is soaked. Let mixture set for about 45 minutes, patting the bread down into the liquid occasionally. Begin baking at low heat with 14 briquets on top and 6 on the bottom for 40 minutes. Then increase briquets to 21 on top and 10 on the bottom and bake for 15 minutes longer or until well browned and puffy.

Serve with warm sauce.

- Exploradores Dutch Oven Team
Bill & Cindy Williamson
Allen, TX

Desserts

Lemon-Pecan Custard Squares
12 inch Dutch oven - Serves 8 - 12

¼ cup butter or margarine, softened
1/3 cup powdered sugar
1½ cups flour
½ cup pecans, finely chopped
3 eggs
1½ cups sugar
3 Tbsp flour
1/3 cup lemon juice
grated peel of one lemon
additional powdered sugar to sprinkle on top
lemon slices and pecan halves for garnish

- Light enough charcoal for **2 & 1/2 rings*** plus 10 briquets.
- Mix butter, 1/3 cup powdered sugar, and 1½ cups flour until crumbly. Add pecans and blend again.
- Place mixture into lightly oiled 12 inch Dutch oven. Pat mixture firmly and evenly into bottom of oven creating a slightly raised (½ inch) collar around outside edge. (Putting powdered sugar on hands keeps dough from sticking to hands.) Place oven over **1 ring*** of freshly lit charcoal. Cover with lid and add **1½ rings*** of freshly lit charcoal to lid. Bake 15 to 20 minutes, until crust is lightly browned.
- While crust is cooking prepared the custard filling. Put eggs into mixing bowl and beat. Then add sugar, 3 Tbsp flour, lemon juice and lemon peel. Mix well.
- When crust is golden, stir custard mixture and pour on top of crust. Make sure pot is level. Cover with lid and continue cooking 15 - 20 minutes more. Turn pot once.
- Remove from heat and set lid aside. Sift powdered sugar on top, according to taste, while still hot. Garnish with lemon slices and pecan halves.

Lemon squares are best when they have _cooled at least 45 minutes._

- Dos Dinwiddies
Duane & Sandy Dinwiddie
Houston, TX

*See 'Dinwiddie Method of Charcoal Briquet Use' on page 10.

Medina Apple Bread Pudding
12 inch Dutch oven

8 - 10 Medina apples	¾ cup brown sugar
12 slices white bread	1 tsp cinnamon
2 sticks (1 cup) butter	12 eggs
1½ cups pecans	½ cup raisins
¾ cup sugar	hot maple syrup

Chop apples - sauté apple with 1 stick butter, ¼ cup sugar, ¼ cup brown sugar and cinnamon until apples start to get soft. Remove from heat and add raisins. Set aside.

Butter bread on one side - place 6 pieces butter side down in Dutch oven - top with apple mixture and pecans. Place the other 6 pieces of bread butter side down on top of apple mixture. Mix eggs and pour over bread. Let sit for 5 minutes. Cook about 350°F, using **1 ring*** on the bottom and **1½ rings*** on the top for 30 minutes or until top starts to brown & eggs are set. Top with hot maple syrup.

- Winnie & Lynn Evans
Houston, TX

*See 'Dinwiddie Method of Charcoal Briquet Use' on page 10.

Nana's Hermits
12 inch Dutch oven - Yield 30 cookies

1 cup shortening	1½ tsp cinnamon
2 cups brown sugar	1 tsp cloves
2 eggs	½ tsp baking soda
1 cup sour milk (sweet milk with 1 tsp vinegar added)	
2 2/3 cups flour	1 cup raisins
½ cup nuts	1 cup apples, chopped (optional)

Pre-heat Dutch oven with 8 - 10 coals on the bottom and 14 - 16 coals on top.

Cream shortening and sugar, add eggs, then milk. Blend well. Mix dry ingredients, add to wet mixture. Stir in nuts and apples. Drop by rounded tablespoon on the bottom of a foil lined 12 Dutch oven. Bake for 15 minutes. These cookies are soft and cake-like.

Historical Note

Saturday, was Nana's baking day. Anyone who came to visit would be greeted by the smell of apple pie baking and sometimes the spicy sweet aroma of these cookies. Nana wouldn't bother making individual cookies, she would spread the soft dough in long 2 inch wide strips in two rows on her cookie sheets and would then slice the resulting 4 inch wide strips into 2 inch bars.

- Nancy Alemany
Sugar Land, TX

Pineapple Bread Pudding with Sauce
12 inch Dutch oven - Serves 8 - 12

1 long loaf French Bread	1 tsp vanilla
3½ cups milk	½ cup white raisins
2 cups sugar	4 eggs, lightly beaten
1 - 8 oz can crushed pineapple, undrained	

Grease oven liberally with butter. Tear bread into bite size pieces. to make 4 - 5 cups. Place bread into a large mixing bowl and cover with milk. Allow bread to absorb milk then add sugar, vanilla, raisins, pineapple and eggs. Stir gently to mix ingredients. Pour into greased Dutch oven and bake at 350°F about 1 hour. Use 10 coals on the bottom and 15 coals on the lid. The top should be golden brown and crusty around the edges. Ladle pineapple sauce over top and serve warm.

Pineapple Bread Pudding with Sauce continued......

Pineapple Bread Pudding with Sauce continued.....

SAUCE

½ cup butter
1 cup sugar
½ tsp cinnamon
juice of ¼ of lemon
1 tsp vanilla
1 - 8 oz can crushed pineapple

In a small pan, melt butter and add sugar. Stir over low heat until sugar dissolves. Add next four ingredients and bring to a boil. Pour over pudding white still hot.

- Shem & Norma Ray
Sulphur Springs, TX

Pioneer Pudding
12 inch Dutch oven

2 cups bread cubes
2 cups milk
2 Tbsp butter
¼ to ½ cup sugar, to taste
2 eggs
dash of salt
1 tsp vanilla

- Scald the milk with the butter and sugar in the Dutch oven.
- Meanwhile, cut day old bread, crusts and all, into ½ inch cubes and place in a bowl.
- Take the pot with the scalded milk from the hot coals and allow to cool slightly.
- Beat eggs slightly.
- Add salt and vanilla to cooling milk and stir. Then add slightly beaten eggs to milk, stirring constantly. Stir bread cubes into milk mixture.
- Replace lid tightly and return Dutch oven to coals. Bake for about one hour with moderate heat, using 10 coals on the bottom and 15 coals evenly distributed on the lid.
- Pudding is done when a small knife inserted in the center of the pudding comes out clean.

Note

If you wish, add ½ tsp cinnamon or nutmeg along with the salt and vanilla. Or you may add ¼ cup coconut. You may wish to spread you favorite jetty, jam or orange marmalade on the top of the baked pudding.

- Bill & Marilyn D'Lizarraga
Sulphur Springs, TX

Plain Ol' Pumpkin Bread Puddin'
12 inch Dutch oven - Serves 12

12 slices bread, cubed & dried
1 - 30 oz can pumpkin, solid pack
1½ cups sugar
1 tsp salt
1 tsp ginger
½ tsp ground cloves
1 tsp mace
1 tsp vanilla
½ cup walnuts, coarsely chopped
6 eggs, well beaten
6 cups whole milk
4 Tbsp butter, unsalted

Heat Dutch oven to 350° F, using **1 ring*** of coals on the bottom and **1½ rings*** of coals on the top. Beat eggs well, add milk, and vanilla while constantly stirring. Mix dry ingredients together - the sugar, salt, ginger, cloves, and mace. Stir the dry mixture into the egg mixture. Then stir in the pumpkin until all is well mixed. Add dried bread cubes and pour all into the preheated oven.

When pudding is almost cooked, dot crust with butter. Bake for 55 - 60 minutes or until inserted knife comes out clean.

Plain Ol' Pumpkin Bread Puddin' continued. . . . .

Plain Ol' Pumpkin Bread Puddin' continued.....

Historical Note

Bein' tarred of plain ol' bread puddin', day after day, out on the range. . . . we come acrost a bunch of big ol' pumkins jes agrowin' like mad - way out in the middle of no whar. . . . so we plucked us a few, and we made all kinds of pumkin stuff out of them, includin' this "Plain Ol' Pumkin Bread Puddin". It shore beat Plain Ol' Bread Puddin'!

- Bungy Hartshorn
Bandera, TX

*See 'The Dinwiddie Method of Charcoal Briquet Use' on page 10.

Notes

Pies & Cobblers

Apple Custard Pie
12 inch Dutch oven - Serves 12

3 cups all-purpose flour
1 tsp salt
1 cup butter
6 medium apples, sliced & peeled
1 1/3 cups sugar
2 tsp cinnamon
2 large eggs
1 cup sugar
2 cups evaporated whole milk

For crust, mix flour, salt and butter with fork until mixture resembles coarse meal. Press firmly on the bottom and sides of buttered 12 inch Dutch oven. Place sliced apples on crust. Sprinkle with 1 cup and 2 Tbsp sugar and 2 tsp cinnamon. Bake with 14 coals on the bottom and 20 coals on top for 20 minutes. Beat eggs, 7/8 cup (1 cup minus 2 Tbsp) sugar, and 2 cups evaporated milk. Pour over apples, remove half of remaining coals from bottom of oven and bake 30 minutes longer.

- Paul & Sissy Garrison
Medina, TX

Apple Dumplings with Maple-Cider Sauce
12 inch Dutch oven - Serves 8

3 cups all-purpose flour
1 tsp salt
¾ cup butter, chilled & cut into pieces
5 Tbsp shortening
½ cup chilled apple cider
8 Granny Smith apples
½ cup brown sugar, firmly packed
1 cup pecans, chopped
1/3 cup butter, softened
1 egg
1 Tbsp water
4 cinnamon sticks, broken
Maple Cider Sauce

- Combine flour & salt; cut in butter pieces and shortening until mixture is crumbly. Sprinkle chilled cider, 1 Tablespoon at a time, evenly over crumbs. Stir with a fork until dry ingredients are moistened. Shape into 2 (½ inch thick) squares: cover and chill.

- Core each apple, leaving ½ of skin intact on bottom. Peel top two thirds of each apple, set aside.
- Combine brown sugar, & pecans; stir in softened butter, blend well. Spoon evenly into apples. Roll pastry squares to 1/8 th inch thickness on a floured surface; cut each square into 4 (7 inch) squares.
- Press 1 pastry square around each apple; remove excess pastry from bottom of apple.
- Combine egg and water, beat slightly. Brush mixture over apples.
- Place cinnamon stick half in the top of each pastry wrapped apple. Place apples in a slightly greased Dutch oven.
- Bake, using 9 coals on the bottom and 18 coals on top, for 40 minutes. Pour Maple Cider Sauce over apples and bake 15 minutes more.

Maple Cider Sauce

1½ cups apple cider	¼ cup brown sugar, firmly packed
2 tsp cornstarch	
2/3 cup maple syrup	¼ cup fresh lemon juice

Combine cider and cornstarch in a small oven, stirring until smooth. Add remaining ingredients. Bring to a boil - boil 1 minute.

- Exploradores Dutch Oven Team
Bill & Cindy Williamson
Allen, TX

Addy's Peach Cobbler
10 inch Dutch oven - Yields 8 servings

Fruit Filling:
8 cups sliced peaches, fresh or frozen
2 Tbsp flour
½ tsp cinnamon
1 cup sugar

Crust:

1 cup flour	6 Tbsp milk or half and-half
1 Tbsp baking powder	flour for cutting board
¼ tsp salt	1 Tbsp cinnamon
3 Tbsp butter or margarine	1 Tbsp sugar

Mix the peaches with 2 Tbsp flour and cinnamon in a large bowl. Add the sugar a little at a time until the fruit is sweet enough for your taste. Spoon the fruit mixture into a greased Dutch oven.

Sift together flour, sugar, baking powder, and salt into a bowl. Cut the butter into small chunks and add to flour mixture. Use a pastry cutter to blend flour mixture into pea-sized lumps. Add milk. Stir with a fork until all ingredients are moistened.

Roll dough out on a flour covered table to ¼ inch thick. Cut crust into shapes and place on top of fruit mixture. Mix cinnamon and sugar and sprinkle over the crust.

Bake with **1 ring*** of coals underneath and **2 rings*** of coal on lid for 30 - 35 minutes.

- The Cherokee Chefs
Bonita & Felicia Sanders
Seabrook, TX

*See ' The Dinwiddie Method of Charcoal Briquette Use' on page 2.

Pies & Cobbler

Apple Crisp from the Lodge of "Twin Points"
12 inch Dutch oven - Serves 8

6 Granny Smith apples (5 - 6 cups)
1 cup sugar
2 Tbsp flour
½ tsp nutmeg
1 tsp cinnamon
2 tsp butter

1 & 1/3 cups flour, sifted
1 cup brown sugar, packed
1 tsp cinnamon
pinch of baking soda
pinch of salt
½ cup butter, cold

Pare and slice apples. Toss in a bowl with next four ingredients. Set aside.
Combine remaining ingredients in a separate bowl. Cut in cold butter with 2 knives.

Preheat Dutch oven in fire pit for approximately 10 minutes.

Pour apple mixture into Dutch oven. Dot with small blobs of butter.

Pour dry mixture over top of apples and press down slightly.

Place Dutch oven in the pit. If using briquets, place 12 briquets on the bottom, and 30 on the lid. If using 2 inch oak limbs, use six inches of wood coals on the bottom and 18 inches of wood coals on the lid. If using a 10 inch oven, reduce the coals by 30 to 40 %.

Cook until done (approximately 45 minutes).

Serve warm with whipped cream if available.

- The cooking team of
Jerry Parra & Barbara Stiranka
Houston, TX

Apple Delight
12 inch Dutch oven - Serves 6

4 medium apples (Granny Smith)
½ cup butter
1 cup sugar
2 Tbsp cinnamon
½ cup water
¼ cup flour

Peel and slice apples (approximately 3/8 inch thick). Place in a well oiled Dutch oven and add the water. Sprinkle with cinnamon. Using a pastry blender or 2 knives, blend the sugar, flour and butter until crumbly. Spread over apple mixture. Place 8 charcoal briquets under Dutch oven and 15 charcoal briquets on top of Dutch oven. Check after 1½ hours. Apples should be soft.

- Tom Payne

Blackberry Cobbler
14 inch Dutch oven - Serves 14 - 18 people

6 cups all-purpose flour
2 tsp salt
2½ cups shortening
2 eggs, well beaten
10 Tbsp cold water
2 Tbsp apple cider vinegar

Combine flour and salt, cut in shortening until mixture resembles coarse meal. Combine eggs, water and vinegar. Mix well and stir into flour mixture. Turn pastry out onto a lightly floured surface, knead until you have a good texture. Set aside 1/3 of the pastry for the top of the cobbler. Roll out the rest of the pastry on a floured surface to ¼ inch thickness, approximately 3 - 4 inches larger than the lid of the Dutch oven. Place the pastry in a well greased 14 inch Dutch oven, pressing the pastry evenly up the sides of the oven. *(Hint: it may be easier to cut the pastry in quarters and place it in the oven so that the pieces overlap and then press them back together.)*

Pies & Cobbler

FILLING

8 cups fresh blackberries
3½ cup sugar
½ cup all-purpose flour
1 tsp or more of vanilla to taste

Combine all of the above in a large bowl and stir until well mixed. Let stand for 30 minutes, or until a sufficient amount of juice is created. (If blackberries are not juicy enough, mash them up a little or add 1 cup of water at a time until it looks right.) Pour into the pastry lined Dutch oven. On a floured board roll our reserved pastry to approximately the size of the Dutch oven lid. Cut pastry into 3/4 inch wide strips and arrange in a lattice design over filling. Moisten ends of pastry strips and press to the side of the bottom pastry to seal. Dot the top of the cobbler with ¼ inch thick pads of butter (about one stick of butter) and sprinkle with 2 - 4 Tbsp of sugar and cinnamon to taste.

Cook at approximately 350°F until lightly brown (about 1 hour). Start with 8 - 10 coals on the bottom and 14 - 16 coals on the top.

Historical Note

This recipe is a variation of a basic cobbler recipe by Jewel Garrison of Medina, TX. Her original cobbler recipe was handed down to her from her mother and was published in "Southern Living Magazine" in 1989. Her original cobbler recipe is well over 100 years old.

- The Hatfield Ranch Cocineros cooking team
Dan Hatfield & Cindy Rather
Medina, TX

Blackberry Dutch Pie
10 inch Dutch oven - Serves 6 - 8

PIE CRUST For two crust pie:
- ½ cup boiling water
- 1½ cup shortening
- 2 Tbsp milk
- 4 cups flour
- 2 tsp salt

Whip with a beater or by hand, ½ cup boiling water, 1½ cups shortening, 2 Tbsp milk until smooth and thick. Add 4 cups flour, 2 tsp salt and blend well. Roll or pat out on a floured surface to the needed size (2 inches larger than the bottom of the Dutch oven).

PIE FILLING:
- 1½ cups sugar
- 2 cups blackberries, (fresh, frozen or canned in water)
- 4 Tbsp water
- 1 Tbsp butter or margarine

Blend sugar and flour. Mix in blackberries (fresh is best) with butter or margarine.

Grease and flour the bottom of a 10 inch Dutch oven. Place the rolled out dough in the oven so it extends 1 to 1½ inches up the side. Pour in the filling and dot with butter, add top crust and seal to bottom crust at sides. Place lid on the Dutch oven. Bake with 7 briquets on the bottom and 14 briquets on the lid (350°F).

Bake for 20 minutes then add 7 more briquets to the lid of the oven. Bake until done about 45 - 50 minutes. Let cool before serving.

- The Chuckle Wagon Cookers
Steve & Jeanice Bias
La Marque, TX

Buttermilk Pie

12 inch Dutch oven - Serves 8

3 cups all-purpose flour
1¼ cups vegetable shortening
1 tsp salt
1 large egg, well beaten
5 Tbsp water
1 Tbsp vinegar

1 stick butter (½ cup)
6 large eggs
3 cups sugar
½ cup all-purpose flour
1 tsp vanilla extract
1 cup buttermilk

CRUST: Cut shortening into flour and salt. Combine 1 egg, water, and vinegar. Pour into flour mix all at once. Blend with a spoon just until flour is all moistened. This is an easy crust to handle and can be re-rolled without toughening. Roll out crust and place in bottom of 12 inch Dutch oven. (Crust also keeps in refrigerator for up to two weeks.)

FILLING: In a Dutch oven, melt and brown one stick of butter. Pour into a bowl and set aside to cool. Beat 6 eggs well, add 3 cups sugar, ½ cup flour, vanilla, buttermilk, and melted butter. Mix well and pour filling into pie shell and bake 45 minutes with 15 coals on the bottom and 25 coals on the top.

- Paul & Sissy Garrison
Medina, TX

Caramel Crunch Apple Pie

30 vanilla caramels
1 cup flour
4 cups apples, sliced
½ cup sugar or brown sugar
¼ cup chopped nuts

2 Tbsp water
½ tsp cinnamon
1 unbaked 10 inch pie shell
½ cup butter

In a double boiler, melt caramels. Layer apples and melted caramels in the pie shell. Then combine flour, sugar and cinnamon.

Caramel Crunch Apple Pie continued. . . . .

Caramel Crunch Apple Pie continued. . . . .
Cut in butter until mixture is crumbly. Stir in nuts. Sprinkle over top of pie. Bake in a hot Dutch oven. Cover the top of Dutch oven with coals. Place 11 coals underneath.

PLAIN PASTRY

1½ cups all-purpose flour   ½ cup shortening
¼ tsp salt   4 to 5 Tbsp water

Sift the flour and salt together into a mixing bowl. Cut shortening into flour with a pastry cutter or fork until pastry is walnut size. Add the water and toss, however only long enough to bind the pastry. Roll out into a 1/8 inch to 1/4 inch circle and place in a 10 inch pie pan.

- Jimma & Shannon Morris
Austin, Arkansas

Cherry Pecan Cobbler
12 inch Dutch Oven - Serves 6 - 8

3 pie crusts, cut into 1 inch strips (to make 3 separate layers of crust)
½ cup sugar
1½ tsp cinnamon
1 cup pecans, broken into small pieces
3 - 21 oz cans, cherry pie filling

1. Using your favorite homemade pie crust recipe, frozen deep-dish pie crusts, or the kind made from a box, roll out the three pie crusts and cut into 1 inch strips.

2. Lightly oil Dutch oven and set up to cook with 8 briquets on the bottom.

Pies & Cobbler

3. Cover the bottom of oven with the strips of 1 (one) pie crust. Mix the sugar and cinnamon together and sprinkle 1/3 of mixture lightly over the crust.

4. Pour 1 (one) can of cherry pie filling over crust, spreading evenly. Sprinkle ½ cup pecans over filling.

5. Repeat steps 3 and 4 with the other two pie crusts, and cans of filling, reversing the direction of the pie crust strips, and sprinkling pecans and cinnamon sugar mixture over second layer, and only cinnamon-sugar over top layer.

6. Cover and bake for 1½ hours with 17 briquets on the top lid and 8 briquets underneath. Bake until cobbler is golden brown and bubbling.

7. Remove lid. Let cool for ten minutes or so; then serve with ice cream, whipped cream, or your preference.

Historical Note

Recipe adapted from *Dutch Oven Cooking with Tony Cano* by Tony Cano and Ann Sochat. Published by Tony Cano Enterprises, PO Box 220205, El Paso, TX 79913.

- The Oven Lovin' Team
Judy & Jamie Ragland
Duncanville, TX

Crunchy Apples
12 inch Dutch oven - Serves 12 - 15

2 cans apple pie filling
1½ cups flour
¼ tsp salt
½ cup brown sugar, packed
1½ sticks (¾ cup) butter
½ cup brandy (optional)

½ cup pecans, chopped
½ cup oatmeal, regular
½ tsp baking soda
½ cup white sugar
½ cup raisins

Crunchy Apples continued. . . . .

Crunchy Apples continued. . . . .
FILLING:
Pour apple pie filling into slightly oiled oven. Stir in raisins (Note: the raisins are delicious when well soaked in brandy before adding to the apples.)

TOPPING:
In a bowl, mix dry ingredients together - flour, salt, brown & white sugar, oats and baking soda. Cut in the butter with a pastry blender until well mixed to a granular texture. Sprinkle over top of apples, even out to smooth. Sprinkle chopped nuts on top.

Cook 1 hour or until topping is done (crisp, browned and firm). Bake at 350° F using 8 - 10 coals under for first 10 - 15 minutes and 14 coals on top. Remove bottom coals after 10 - 15 minutes and continue with top heat.

Historical Note
This old timer is just a variation of the simple cobbler that didn't take too much time for the chuck wagon "cookie's". Grandmother did a good job and improved it with the 'crisp' idea from which this recipe evolved.

- Larry & Bungy Hartshorn
Bandera, TX

Dutch Oven Cherry Pie
12 inch Dutch oven

1 bag frozen cherries
sugar to taste

2 pie crusts
2 tin (not aluminum) pie pans

Heat oven over coals. Prepare pie crusts if not already done. Insert one pie pan in oven. Add sugar to cherries and let sit until thawed. Line remaining pie pan with one crust and fill with cherries. Cover with remaining crust and poke hole in it with a fork. Place in oven

Pies & Cobbler

and cover lid with hot coals. Check when you first begin to smell the pie and then periodically after that. Pie is done when crust in golden brown and filling is bubbly.

Note
As with everything you cook in a Dutch oven, if using a wood fire, rotate the oven periodically to evenly distribute the heat.

Grandma 20's Apple Brown Betty
12 inch Dutch oven - Serves 10 - 12

Mix together:
> 6 cups tart apples, peeled cored and sliced
> ½ cup sugar

Spread evenly over bottom of Dutch oven

Top with:
> 1 cup brown sugar
> 1 cup oats
> ¼ cup flour
> ½ cup butter, softened
> 1 cup pecans, chopped
> 2 tsp cinnamon
> 1 tsp nutmeg

Bake using 8 charcoal briquets on the bottom and 13 briquets on the top for 20 minutes. Remove from bottom heat. Continue cooking until apples are tender and topping is brown. Serve with ice cream or heavy cream poured over the top.

Historical Note
When I was small my grandma fixed this for me as often as I asked. Her Dutch oven was just a little different than the ones I use, hers went into the oven (it had been my great grandmother's). The Dutch
Grandma 20's Apple Brown Betty continued.....

Grandma 20's Apple Brown Betty continued. . . . .

oven had no legs and the lid was dome shaped with no lip. I grew up thinking any black pot that was big and deep was a Dutch oven and could produce some great food.

- The Ewings
Allen, TX

Jiffy Fruit Cobbler
12 inch Dutch oven - Serves 10

1 cup butter
2 cups all-purpose flour
2 cups sugar
4 tsp baking powder
½ tsp salt

1½ cups milk
3 cups your favorite fruit
½ tsp pepper
1½ tsp nutmeg

Melt butter in 12 inch Dutch oven. Mix flour, milk, sugar, baking powder, salt, nutmeg and pepper until smooth. Pour into melted butter, stirring gently. Add fruit without stirring again. Bake with 15 coals on bottom and 20 coal on top of the Dutch oven for 30 - 45 minutes or until crust is browned

- Casey & Courtney Garrison
Medina, TX

Medina Apple Fest Apple Cobbler
12 inch Dutch oven

CRUST:
- 2 cups flour
- 1 cup shortening (butter flavored Crisco®)
- ¼ tsp salt
- 3½ Tbsp water

Cut flour and shortening together using a pastry blender or 2 knives until mixture is in pea size chunks. Add water slowly and mix each addition with a fork until mixture forms a ball. Divide in half and roll out on floured surface or between wax paper. Fit into baking dish. Cut lattice strips for the top crust.

FILLING:
- 2 cups sugar
- 1½ tsp cinnamon
- 1½ Tbsp flour
- ½ tsp nutmeg
- 4 - 5 apples, peeled, cored & sliced

Line bottom crust with half of the sugar, cinnamon, flour and nutmeg. Fill dish with sliced apples and add rest of sugar spice mixture. Place dish on a rack in bottom of oven. Bake at 400°F for 15 minutes, using 19 coals on the top and 10 coals on the bottom. Finish cooking at 375°F using 17 coals on the top and 8 coals on the bottom for 45 minutes or until apples are soft.

- Wayne Switzer
Joshua, TX

Mock Apple Pie
10 inch Dutch oven - Serves 6 - 8

CRUST:
- 3 cups flour
- 1½ tsp salt
- 1 cup plus 2 Tbsp Crisco®
- 6 Tbsp water

FILLING:
- 36 Ritz® crackers
- 2 cups water
- 2 cups sugar
- 2 tsp cream of tartar
- 2 Tbsp lemon juice
- grated rind of one lemon
- ½ stick, butter or margarine
- cinnamon, to taste

- Mix flour & salt in a large bowl
- Cut in Crisco® until mixture is uniform and very fine.
- Mix in water
- Roll out on floured board.
- Use 2/3's of crust to cover bottom and sides of oven.
- Break Ritz® crackers coarsely into oven.
- Combine water, sugar and cream of tartar in sauce pan; boil gently for 15 minutes.
- Add lemon juice and rind in sauce pan, mix together, let cool.
- Pour sauce pan syrup over crackers. Dot generously with butter or margarine and sprinkle with cinnamon.
- Cover top with rest of crust, trimming and fluting edges together.
- Cut slits into crust to let steam escape, sprinkle crust with cinnamon.
- Bake at 425°F for 30 - 35 minutes, until crust is crisp and golden, with 9 briquets underneath and 18 on top. Watch closely during last 10 minutes to avoid burning crust.
- Serve warm!

Historical Note

This is an old recipe published by the maker of Ritz® Crackers that we both can remember our mother and relatives using back when we

Pies & Cobbler

were youngsters. It's hard to tell that there are not real apples in this pie!

- The Two B's Dutch Oven Team
Bill & Beverly Brummel
San Antonio, TX

Pinto Bean Pie
10 inch Dutch oven - Serves 6 - 8

CRUST:
- ¼ cup boiling water
- ¾ cup shortening
- 1 Tbsp milk
- 2 cups flour
- 1 tsp salt

Whip with a beater or by hand the boiling water, shortening and milk until smooth and thick. Add flour and salt and blend well. Roll or pat out on floured surface to the needed size (2 inches larger that the bottom of the Dutch oven).

In a well greased and floured Dutch oven, place the rolled out dough so it extends 1 to 1½ inches up the side of oven.

FILLING:
- 1 cup sugar
- 1 cup milk
- ½ cup pecans
- 1 tsp allspice
- 1 tsp vanilla
- 1 tsp cinnamon
- 2 egg yolks
- 3 Tbsp flour
- 1 cup mashed pinto beans (very smooth)

Blend sugar, flour, cinnamon and allspice together. Mix in milk and eggs. Add pinto beans (mashed very smooth), pecans and vanilla, mix well. Pour into unbaked pie shell and place lid on the Dutch oven. Bake at 350°F, using 7 briquets on the bottom and 14 briquets on the lid. Bake for 30 minutes then add more briquets to the lid of the Dutch oven. Bake until done (45 - 50 minutes). Let cool before serving.
Pinto Bean Pie continued. . . . .

Pinto Bean Pie continued. . . . .

For a 14 inch Dutch oven double the recipe and place the Dutch oven over 11 briquets and place 21 briquets on the lid.

> - The Chuckle Wagon Cookers
> Steve & Jeanice Bias
> La Marque, TX

Pioneer "Lemon" Meringue Pie with Raisins
12 inch Dutch oven - Serves 10 - 12

FILLING:
- 1½ cups raisins
- boiling water to soften raisins
- 4 cups sugar
- 9 Tbsp cornstarch
- 9 Tbsp all-purpose flour
- 9 slightly beaten egg <u>yolks</u>
- 6 Tbsp butter or margarine
- ¼ cup cider vinegar
- 1 baked 12 inch pastry shell, cooled

PASTRY:
- 4 cups all-purpose flour
- 1½ tsp salt
- 1 1/3 cups shortening
- 10 - 14 Tbsp cold water

MERINGUE:
- 9 egg whites
- 1½ tsp cream of tartar
- 1 1/3 cups sugar

FILLING: Cover raisins with boiling water to soften; cool. Drain. In saucepan mix sugar, cornstarch, flour, and dash of salt. Stir in 4½ cups water. Cook and stir over high heat till boiling. Reduce heat; cook and stir 2 minutes more. Remove from heat. Stir moderate amount hot mixture into egg yolks; return to hot mixture in sauce pan. Bring to boiling; cook and stir 2 minutes. Add butter. Slowly stir in vinegar. Stir in raisins. Pour into pastry shell. Spread Meringue over hot filling, sealing to edge of pastry. Bake at 350°F for 12 - 15 minutes.

PASTRY: Stir flour and salt together; cut in shortening with pastry blender till pieces are size of small peas. Sprinkle 1 Tbsp water over part of mixture. Gently toss with a fork; push to side of bowl. Repeat till all is moistened. Form ball. Flatten on lightly floured surface by pressing with edge of hand 3 times across in both directions. Roll from center to edge till 1/8 th inch thick. Fit pastry into bottom of oven; trim around edge; fold under and flute edge. Prick bottom and sides well with fork. Bake at 450°F till golden, 10 to 12 minutes. Cool before using.

MERINGUE: Beat 9 egg whites with 1½ tsp vanilla and 3/4 tsp cream of tartar till soft peaks form. Gradually add 1 1/3 cups sugar, beating till stiff peaks form and sugar is dissolved.

Historical Note

The first women on the frontier lacked many cooking ingredients that they had been used to back East. One of these was lemon juice. Not to be outdone by the hardships of frontier life, these resourceful women developed a recipe for lemon pie using homemade apple cider vinegar instead of lemon juice. This 'Pioneer Mock Lemon Pie with Raisins' is an excellent authentic example of one of these early pies.

- Larry & Bungy Hartshorn
Bandera, TX

Spring Blush Fruit Pie
12 inch Dutch oven - Serves 10 - 12

1 pie crust portion "Never Fail Pie Crust"
½ cup orange juice
2 Tbsp Grand Mariner
1 cup dried cherries or cranberries
Spring Blush Fruit Pie continued. . . . .

Spring Blush Fruit Pie continued.....
¼ cup snipped dried apricots
¾ cup sugar
2 Tbsp flour
1 Tbsp orange peel, finely shredded
3 cups apples, thinly sliced & peeled
Crumb Topping

- Prepare and roll out pie crust to 2 inches larger than Dutch oven. Fold crust in quarters, place in oven and fit to bottom and side of oven. Trim and crimp top edge of crust.

- For filling; in 8 inch oven over 10 coals, heat orange juice and Grand Mariner to boiling. Add cranberries or cherries and apricots. Remove from heat and let stand 10 minutes or until fruit is softened; do not drain. In large mixing bowl stir together sugar, flour, and orange peel. Add apples and the undrained fruit, then gently mix until coated. Transfer fruit mixture to the pastry-lined oven.

- Cover with Crumb topping or top with pie crust as preferred. Place over 10 coals, cover and add 14 coals to top of lid. Bake for 20 minutes. Check crust for browning. Bake 25 - 30 more minutes.

NEVER FAIL PIE CRUST

6 cups flour
2 cups Crisco®
1 Tbsp salt

1 egg
2 Tbsp white vinegar
water

In a large bowl, mix flour, Crisco®, and salt with a pastry blender until size of small peas. Break egg into measuring cup, beat slightly. Finish filling cup with cold water to the one cup line. Add vinegar and sprinkle the liquids over the dry ingredients. Mix well. Pie crust can be re-rolled and is tender and easy to handle. Makes 6 pie crusts. Use only amount of crust needed. Will keep 3 weeks in refrigerator, also freezes well.

CRUMB TOPPING

½ cup rolled oats
½ cup flour
½ cup packed brown sugar

¼ tsp cinnamon
¼ tsp butter (no substitutes)
¼ cup chopped pecans

In medium bowl combine oats, flour, sugar, and cinnamon. Cut in butter with pastry blender until crumbly. Stir in nuts. Spoon over pie filling and bake as directed.

- The Oven Lovin' Team
Judy & Jamie Ragland
Duncanville, TX

Sourdough Cherry Cobbler
12 inch Dutch oven

1 cup flour
½ cup brown sugar
2 cups sugar
½ tsp cinnamon

½ cup butter
½ cup sourdough starter
1 can cherries

Cook cherries and 1½ cups sugar & ½ cup flour until juice is thick

Mix remainder of flour, brown sugar, ½ cup sugar and cinnamon together.

Cut in butter with a pastry blender, or 2 knives, until crumbly. Add sourdough starter. Spoon over top of cherries and bake for about 1 hour, using 10 coals on the bottom and 12 coals on the top of oven.

- Beverly Modgling
Medina, TX

Surprise Buttermilk Pie
14 inch Dutch oven - Serves 6 - 8

½ cup butter or margarine
2 cups sugar
3 Tbsp flour
3 eggs
1 cup buttermilk

1 cup shredded coconut (This is the surprise part.)
1 tsp vanilla extract
1 unbaked 9 inch pastry shell

Cream butter, gradually add sugar, beating well. Add flour and beat until smooth. Add eggs, beat until blended. Add buttermilk and vanilla, beat well. Place pie dough into 9 inch pie pan and pour pie mixture into pan. Place pie pan inside 14 inch Dutch oven about 1 inch off the bottom (use a cake rack or trivet). Bake in a hot Dutch oven for 45 minutes or until set. Let cool completely.

Instructions for a Hot Dutch oven (400°F):
29 charcoal briquets - Place 2/3 of coals on top of Dutch oven and 1/3 coals on bottom of the Dutch oven.

- Alan & Wayne Switzer
Fort Worth, TX

Peach Cobbler
14 inch Dutch oven - Serves 14 - 18 people

PASTRY:
6 cups all-purpose flour
2 tsp salt
2½ cups shortening

2 eggs, well beaten
10 Tbsp cold water
2 Tbsp apple cider vinegar

Combine flour and salt. Cut in shortening until mixture resembles coarse meal. Combine eggs, water and vinegar. Mix well and stir into flour mixture. Turn pastry out onto a lightly floured surface, knead until you have a good texture. Set aside 1/3 of the pastry for the top of the cobbler. Roll out the rest of the pastry on a floured

Pies & Cobbler

surface to ¼ inch thickness, approximately 3 to 4 inches larger than the lid of the Dutch oven. Place the pastry in a well greased 14 inch Dutch oven, pressing the pastry evenly up the sides of the oven. *(Hint: It may be easier to cut the pastry in quarters and place it in the oven so that the pieces overlap and then press them back together.)*

FILLING:
8 cups fresh peaches, sliced
2½ cups sugar
½ cup all-purpose flour
1 good shot of amaretto liquor (to taste)
1 tsp vanilla

Combine all of the above in a large bowl and stir until well mixed. Let stand for 30 minutes, or until a sufficient amount of juice is created (if peaches are not juicy enough add 1 cup of water at a time until it looks right). Pour into a pastry lined Dutch oven. On a floured board roll our reserved pastry to approximately the size of the Dutch oven lid. Moisten ends of pastry strips and press to the side of the bottom pastry to seal. Dot the top of the cobbler with 1/3 inch thick pats of butter (about one stick of butter) and sprinkle with 2 - 4 Tbsp sugar and cinnamon to taste.

Cook at approximately 350°F until slightly brown (about 1 hour). Start with 8 to 10 coals on the bottom and 14 - 16 coals on the top.

Historical Note

This recipe is a variation of a basic cobbler recipe by Jewel Garrison of Medina, TX. Her original cobbler recipe was handed down to her from her mother and was published in 'Southern Living Magazine' in 1989. Her original cobbler recipe is well over 100 years old.

- From the Hatfield Ranch Cocineros
Dan Hatfield & Cindy Rather
Medina, TX

Praline Apple Crisp
14 inch Dutch oven - Serves 10
"A topping for ice cream or good all by itself!"

2 cups brown sugar
3 - 4 tsp cinnamon, according to preference
16 green cooking apples, peeled, cored and sliced thin
2 cups coarsely chopped pecans
1 cup butter
2 cups flour
2 cups brown sugar

Combine first four items in oven. Cut butter into flour and brown sugar until crumbly. Sprinkle over apples in oven. Place lid on oven. Put 10 - 12 coals on lid and under oven, spacing evenly. Bake approximately 1 hour or until apples are tender and topping is brown. Sauce should be thick and bubbly. If you like a crispier crust, remove lid and let stand 10 - 15 minutes before serving. Serve warm over ice cream, pound cake or angel food cake.

Note: Preparing all those apples is a lot easier with a good old-fashioned hand-cranked apple peeler.

- The Prairie Kitchen
Cheryel Lemley
Covington, TX

Ruby's Easy Cobbler
10 inch Dutch oven - Serves 6

1 stick (½ cup) butter
1 cup flour
1 cup sugar
1 tsp baking powder
¼ tsp salt
¾ cup sweet milk

Pies & Cobbler

2 lbs peaches, (or 2 - 16 oz cans peaches and juice, if out of season)

Start 18 - 20 charcoal briquets
Melt butter in a 10 inch Dutch oven
Mix dry ingredients and milk into a batter, pour over melted butter.
Carefully pour fruit on top of the batter in oven. DO NOT STIR.
Bake with 8 coals on bottom and 10 coals on top, keep the top coals going for 45 minutes to 1 hour.

Historical Note

Ruby, Susan's mother, had 14 kids and they all lived on a hard scrabble farm in the 'Big Woods' in Wood County, Texas.

When Susan was a little bitty girl, the whole family had to work to supplement their meager existence and to obtain hard cash money. During the fall of the year the whole bunch would leave the farm and travel throughout North and East Texas to pick cotton. Many times they had to camp out, or more often, stay in an abandoned farm house near the cotton fields. All had to pick cotton. Ruby sometimes hauled a nursing baby down the rows in a cotton sack. There was not much time or fancy ingredients available to cook so Ruby developed this easy but tasty dish.

- From "The Out Law Gazette"
Hole in the Wall Press
Captain Joe R. Scott, Editor
Susan Scott, Assistant Editor
Sulphur Springs, TX

Susan's Texas Pie
10 inch Dutch oven - Serves 6 - 8

2 sticks butter (in all)	1 box yellow cake mix
1 - 21 oz can cherry pie filling	1 cup shredded coconut
1 can crushed pineapple	1 cup chopped pecans

Susan's Texas Pie continued. . . . .

Lone Star Dutch Oven Society Cookbook

Susan's Texas Pie continued. . . . .
Start 18 - 20 charcoal briquets.

Melt 1 stick butter in a 10 inch Dutch oven. Pour cherries into pot on top of melted butter.

Pour pineapple on top of that. Mix the cake mix with the pineapple juice and pour on top. Spread pecan & coconut on top. Melt second stick of butter and pour on top of all.

Bake with 8 coals on bottom and 10 coals on top, keep the top coals going for 45 minutes to 1 hour.

Historical Note
See historical Note at the end of Ruby's Easy Cobbler.

- From "The Out Law Gazette"
Hole in the Wall Press
Captain Joe R. Scott, Editor
Susan Scott, Assistant Editor
Sulphur Springs, TX

Taste of Texas Apple Cobbler
12 inch Dutch oven - Makes 8 - 10 generous servings

3 cups Pioneer® Low Fat Biscuit & Baking mix
1½ quarts - Love Creek Orchards Apple Pie in a Jar®
1 cup Texas pecans, chopped
1 stick (½ cup) Hill Country Fare® margarine
1 cup Imperial® sugar
Bolner's Fiesta ® brand cinnamon, to taste.

Place oven over 17 bottom briquets to preheat.

Pour apple mix and pecans into oven and stir to combine. Spread 2 cups of baking mix over apples. Put lid on top, add 8 fresh briquets to lid, bake for about 30 minutes.

Pies & Cobbler

Remove lid, mix oven's contents, smooth out mix, sprinkle rest of baking mix over apple mixture, sprinkle cinnamon over contents of oven (as much as you like), and put pats of butter all over.

Remove 10 old briquets from under oven and place on top of lid. Replace lid and cook until top forms a tannish brown crust.
Spoon cobbler into bowls, cover with either milk or ice cream, and enjoy!

Historical Note
This is a variation of a most popular "Dump Cake Cobbler" recipe used and taste tested by hundreds of thousands of Boy Scouts over the past 85 years. Since a Boy Scout is Honest, Helpful, etc., this must be an outstanding recipe!

- The Two B's Dutch Oven Team
Bill & Beverly Brummel
San Antonio, TX

The Two B's Apple Crumble
12 inch Dutch oven - Serves 12 - 16

CRUMBLE:
- 2 cups Pioneer® Low Fat Biscuit & Baking Mix
- 1½ cups brown sugar
- 1 cup pecans, chopped
- 1 cup oats
- ¾ Tbsp cinnamon
- ½ cup margarine

FILLING:
- 4 baking apples, peeled, cored & sliced
- ½ cup sugar
- 1 tsp cinnamon
- 1½ Tbsp all-purpose flour
- vegetable cooking spray

The Two B's Apple Crumble continued. . . . .

The Two B's Apple Crumble continued. . . . .
- Preheat Dutch oven with 10 briquets under oven.
- Blend biscuit mix, brown sugar, pecans and oats in mixing bowl.
- Cut margarine into dry ingredients until pieces are about pea sized.
- Spray inside of oven with a light coating of vegetable oil.
- Spread 1/3 of the oat mixture evenly into bottom of oven.
- Mix apple filling items together and carefully spread over the oat mixture.
- Sprinkle remaining oat mixture over apple mix.
- Sprinkle cinnamon over oat mixture.
- Close oven and place 14 briquets on lid.
- Bake 30 to 35 minutes until done.

Serve warm and enjoy! (Also great chilled and topped with cold low fat yogurt!)

Note

This recipe is an adaptation for use in a 12 inch Dutch oven of the recipe found on the Pioneer Low Fat Biscuit & Baking Mix container. Like most of the recipes we use, this one has been made more "heart healthful" by our using low fat ingredients. For usage in your kitchen oven, set oven for 350°F and use 1/2 of the recipe for an 8" x 8" or 6" x 10" baking pan. Cook for about 30 - 35 minutes or until done.

- The Two B's Dutch Oven Team
Bill & Beverly Brummel
San Antonio, TX

Trail Cobbler
12 inch Dutch oven - Servings 8

2 cups all-purpose flour
1 Tbsp baking powder
¾ tsp salt
½ tsp baking soda
5 Tbsp shortening

2 cups sugar
2 cups milk
1 cup butter, softened
3 cups fruit

Pies & Cobbler

In a large bowl, sift together flour, baking powder, salt and baking soda. Using a pastry blender, or 2 knives, cut the shortening into the flour mixture until coarse crumbs form. Add sugar, milk and butter, mixing well. Add fruit and stir. Bake in a 12 inch Dutch oven. Place 6 - 8 coals under the oven and one ring on top. Bake for about 1 hour or until done. Remove the coals from under the oven and cover the lid with coals to brown the cobbler if desired.

- Todd & Sissie Sandidge
Bandera, TX

Trails End Dream
('A Multi Fruit Cobbler')
12 inch Dutch oven

1 lb dried apricots, quartered
3 Golden Delicious apples, cored, peeled and sliced
½ cup figlets, sliced
1 cup raisins
1 cup pineapple bits
2 cups simple syrup (1 cup water to 2 cups sugar)
½ cup tapioca
2 Tbsp lemon juice
2 Tbsp butter or margarine
1 Tbsp cinnamon
1 tsp nutmeg
1 tsp mace
1 tsp almond extract

TOPPING:
4 cups all-purpose flour
5 Tbsp sugar
2 Tbsp baking powder
½ tsp salt
1½ sticks (¾ cup) butter or margarine
1 1/3 cups milk

Trails End Dream continued. . . . .

Trails End Dream continued.....

- Soak dried fruit until soft (overnight). Drain and reserve liquid.
- In a bowl, mix apricots, figs, raisins, apples, pineapple, simple syrup, tapioca, lemon juice, butter, cinnamon, nutmeg, mace, and almond.
- Pour fruit mixture into a lightly oiled Dutch oven that has been preheated to 400°F. Just cover fruit with reserved liquid. Cook with 12 coals under and 16 coals over until fruit mixture is bubbling. Add topping made as follows:
- In a separate bowl, sift flour, 4 Tbsp sugar, baking powder and salt. Using a pastry blender, cut in butter until texture of coarse meal. Add milk and mix with a fork until dough holds together.
- On a floured surface, pat dough out to ½ inch thickness, then cut into 20 - 2½ inch rounds. Place the rounds on top of fruit, slightly overlapping, on top of the cooking fruit mixture. Sprinkle with the remaining sugar mixed with cinnamon.
- Bake for 30 - 40 minutes or until topping is lightly browned, in a moderate oven, 350°F, using 14 coals on top and 9 coals underneath.

Best served warm, topped with ice cream or whipped cream.

Historical Note

After two months out on the trail, coming back to the ranch always held an element of excitement. No more sleeping between two blankets wherever we camped, no more freezing rain, snow or grub that kept us going but did little more that stave off hunger. Back at the ranch, we had the cozy bunkhouse, warmth AND best of all, the boss's wife (an excellent cook), would fix us a most delicious meal topped off with this dessert.

        - The cooking team of
            Larry Hartshorn & Bill Spangler
            Bandera, TX

Very Berry Cobbler
14 inch Dutch oven

FILLING:
- 2 cups fruit, blueberries, blackberries, or another fruit
- 1 cup sugar
- 1 tsp cinnamon
- ½ tsp ground cloves
- ¼ tsp ginger
- ¼ tsp nutmeg
- 1 tsp lemon extract

Mix sugar and spices into fruit and set aside

- 2 cups hot water
- 2 cups sugar

Dissolve sugar in water and set aside.

CRUST:
- 1½ cups flour
- ½ cup shortening
- 1½ tsp baking powder
- 1/3 cup milk

Mix ingredients well by hand. Roll out into rectangle shape ¼ to ½ inches thick. Spread fruit on dough and roll up jelly roll fashion. Cut into 12 pieces.

Melt ½ cup butter in bottom of 14 inch Dutch oven. Place rolls cut side down in oven. Pour sugar and water mixture over top. Cook at 350 °F (12 briquets on bottom and 16 briquets on top) for one hour.

- Cooking team of
Ike Craddock & Bill Spangler
Medina, TX

Zesty Peach Cobbler
14 inch Dutch oven - Serves 16 - 24

CRUST:
6 cups flour, sifted
¾ cup sugar
1 Tbsp salt
2¼ cups Crisco®, butter flavored
¼ cup ice water
2 eggs, beaten
2 Tbsp vinegar

FILLING:
4 - 29 oz cans sliced peaches, heavy syrup
¾ cup flour
½ cup butter or margarine
1 Tbsp vanilla
1 tsp allspice
1 cup sugar
1 Tbsp cinnamon
1 tsp nutmeg
1/3 cup orange juice concentrate
¼ cup peach liqueur (Heering®)

- Light enough charcoal for a **full spread*** plus 10 briquets.
- Drain peaches, and pour syrup into oiled Dutch oven. Add the remaining filling ingredients, except the peaches.
- Place oven over **full spread*** of coals, with the lid off. Bring to a simmer with frequent stirring and cook until thickened, about 15 minutes total. Pour into a bowl and clean the oven.
- Chop up about a fourth of the peach slices into small pieces, and add all peaches to the thickened filling.
- Prepare the crust dough by:
  combining flour, sugar, salt, and mixing well,
  add water, egg, and vinegar blending well but minimally, then form into a ball (DO NOT KNEAD!)
  chill dough for 1 to 2 hours, if time permits.
- Lightly oil inside of cleaned oven. Start enough charcoal for **3 rings***.
- Divide dough about in half. On lightly floured piece of unbleached muslin, roll out the largest piece of dough to a

Pies & Cobbler

diameter 8 inches larger than the oven. (The muslin greatly improves your ability to get the dough into the oven.) Put rolling pin under muslin until you are centered under the dough and lift up the rolling pin. Gently invert dough into oven and remove muslin. (An extra pair of hands is very helpful.)

- Push dough against bottom and sides of oven, removing any air bubbles. Push upper edges of crust against wall of oven until it remains in upright position. Repair tears with pieces of dough.
- Pour filling into bottom crust and cover with remaining dough that has been rolled out as you did with the bottom crust. Push the two crusts together against the sides of the oven.
- Trim off excess dough and crimp edges of both crusts together against side of oven. Using fingernails and back sides of fingers, push crimped edge of crust down so that it is almost level with top crust.
- Brush on egg wash made of 1 whole egg and 2 Tbsp water with a pastry brush then sprinkle lightly with cinnamon.
- Using a sharp paring knife, cut air vents into crust.
- Bake by setting oven over **1 ring*** and place **1½ rings*** of fresh coals on top for about 50 minutes, until crust is lightly browned and filling is bubbly. If crust is not browned, add charcoal to the lid to finish browning off.

Garnish as desired. Let cool with the lid off for at least 30 minutes before serving. Cobbler will stay hot for an hour.

Historical Note

This is an original filling recipe of ours. The people at Duane's office loved to get our "trial recipes" and they kept suggesting other ingredients. They wanted the cobblers to keep coming for them to sample! The crust is a variation of other vinegar crust recipes.

- Dos Dinwiddies
Duane & Sandy Dinwiddie
Houston, TX

*See 'The Dinwiddie Method of Charcoal Briquet Use' on page 10.

ONE FINAL NOTE

When you have an oven that's either larger or smaller than the recipe you want to try, here are some things to remember:

An 8 inch Dutch oven is half the volume of a 12 inch Dutch oven. A 10 inch Dutch oven is half the volume of a 14 inch Dutch oven. Use a 14 inch Dutch oven when a 9" x 13" pan is called for in baking.

DISCLAIMER

In some instances there were no charcoal instructions with the recipe. In those cases, 'The Dinwiddie Method' was substituted.

Notes